OTHER PUBLICATIONS BY ROXSANE

Timber Talk [as heard in the forests of British Columbia] by E. Joanne Dheilly me, published by Waterwheel Press

Celebrate Japan self-published by Maple Leaf Publishing

Zip [the first 50 years] published by Xlibris

Art and Soul published by Christian Faith Publishing

ZIPPING
ALONG

Enjoy!
Roxsane

ROXSANE TIERNAN

BookVenture Publishing LLC
1000 Country Lane Ste 300
Ishpeming MI 49849
www.bookventure.com
Hotline: 1(877) 276-9751
Fax: 1(877) 864-1686

Ordering Information:
Quantity sales. Special discounts are available on quantity purchases by corporations, associations, and others. For details, contact the publisher at the address above.

Printed in the United States of America.

Library of Congress Control Number	2019933641
ISBN-13: Paperback	978-1-64348-879-0
Pdf	978-1-64348-880-6
ePub	978-1-64348-881-3
Kindle	978-1-64348-882-0

Rev. date: 01/31/2019

ACKNOWLEDGEMENT

I want to acknowledge the help and support of my husband , Bill who is always there for me.--of my daughters, Yvette and Nancy and my grandchildren, Randi, Kori, Kelly, Marcia, and Matt--as well as my siblings,- my cousins-my friends- my students- my homestays- and all the friendly connections I've made through family, Guiding, teaching, Art and traveling. I have been privileged to lead a life full to the brim and I am very grateful. Sincerely, Roxsane K. Tiernan

Since this book is a memoir of my life from 1987 to 2003 I think you need an Introduction unless you know me very well or have read ZIP my previous book that covers the first fifty years of my life, So…

My life has been very full. I am an outgoing person ready to meet new friends; have new experiences. Joining Girl Guides opened many doors for me, so did growing up as the eldest in a family with seven children. There were always chores to do—chopping down trees [1950's]; cutting them up, picking rocks, weeding, picking berries, babysitting, helping to can fruits and vegetables; and whatever other odd jobs there were, were shared by all of us. BUT as I am the eldest by six and a half years the weight on my shoulders was much heavier. By the time I left home at seventeen most of the alder trees we burned for cooking and heat had been cut down, sawed to length and split into burnable pieces by me. My Mom was over burdened with caring for my siblings as babies, toddlers or youngsters as well as cooking, cleaning, doing the laundry and working at whatever outside chore was necessary for our fledgling garden nursery to survive. As a family living on an acreage life was never boring. We all pitched in with the daily tasks.

Guiding took me camping, on community projects, and charitable efforts. School was a haven for me. I graduated out of Grade Eleven by taking Grade Twelve Math, English and Literature in Summer School. After that I moved to Burnaby to take Grade Thirteen overloading my plate [something I still do] with Math 101, Physics 91, and 101, English 100 and 101 [Literature], French 110, History 101, Biology 101 and Chemistry 101. I wanted to be able to succeed no matter which opportunity arose.

Due to my need to support myself I quit school the beginning of May to take a job at Burnaby Orchids as a florist/greenhouse worker. Of course, I got copies of all the old exams I could and studied and studied; applying for scholarships to get me into UBC. I earned two bursaries from the Imperial Daughters of the Empire and the Royal Canadian Legion. That totaled $250. Tuition was $246. I had saved $160 over the summer. Textbooks ate up $75 so I signed up to work for a Jewish family for my room and board. I earned an Interim Elementary Basic Certificate that allowed me to teach. Thank God for that.

I became the principal, teacher, and janitor of a one room ungraded school in a logging camp at Bear Creek on Harrison Lake. There I had six students in Grade One, two in Grade Two, three in Grade Three, three in Grade Four and one in each of Grade Five, Six, Seven and Eight. At nineteen years old I had a lot to learn but I did my best. I remember the first day one of the boys offered me a present so I put out my hand, the frog jumped off but I hadn't reacted so I passed the test. I still have contact with two of my students from that year. In fact I went to their mother's funeral two weeks ago. She was a model parent that showed me how to be the best parent I could be.

At the end of the year I married George who operated the steel spar and we moved into the married quarters of the camp. A new fellow was hired to teach the students. He thought I should do his marking for him. No thanks. I was pregnant and suffering with morning sickness, too. We continued to live in the married quarters until we had two little girls and another on the way. Sometimes little kids need a doctor, too.

We bought the shell of a house in Sardis; put a roof on it, put in windows, doors, added cedar siding and all. I got to plan my kitchen cupboards promising the carpenter I wouldn't change my mind halfway through. We moved in in September. Nancy turned one in October, two and a half year old Yvette came down with pneumonia. Marcia was born in December. George was in camp all week and only home weekends. Now I needed to learn how to drive a car.

We finished the inside of the house gradually; painting the walls and ceilings. We hired a fellow to put in the brick fireplace. George made an ash china cabinet for the dining room and a bookshelf for the living room. I made curtains and sewed most of the girls' and my clothes. We had a garden and planted fruit trees. Once everything was as we wanted it George decided he wanted to live closer to his folks to we put the house up for sale and went looking for a place closer to town.

We moved to the Guildford area just as the shopping center was being built. The house was solidly built but unique. There were a couple of places if you went out you would fall eight feet. The rooms were large—you could have a party in the bathroom. And their color choice was strange greyed purple in the living room, orange in the kitchen. There were lots of windows and beautiful hardwood floors. I painted the walls. George built sundecks and a carport. Soon he wanted to move again. He went out and found a better house in Surrey but I said no. He was working in Squamish if we were going to move we needed to be able to live together. Besides living close to his family wasn't working for me.

I had a system of cleaning and tidying the house before George came home so we could enjoy our time together. Other times I did what worked for me. If the garden needed attention it got it. If I wanted to get the girls doing a craft project I did. George's Dad would arrive whenever and go back tell his wife and daughter how awful a house-wife I was because the beds weren't made by nine thirty or ten. I was relieved when we moved to Squamish after a serious confrontation with his sister. At least George believed in me. He stood up to his sister and his Dad for me. Seems his Dad told him I was having an affair with his uncle. Really!

In Squamish I volunteered as Captain of the local Girl Guide company with the able assistance of Lieutenant Audrey Brown.[1969] In 1977 I was in charge of Handcrafts for 2500 Guides, and Guiders, who came to Cape Breton, Nova Scotia for an International Camp. We lived in Squamish, British Columbia. I chose my staff by telephone from Toronto. They all cooperated—an amazing group. My choices were good. The program was very popular. I learned a lot. There was a lot of resistance from the English speakers to everything being done totally bilingually. As you can imagine it really slows things down. We had girls from Kuwait. The Jewish girls came from France. Their leader seemed picky to me. But our Canadian English and French were the most problematic, I thought.

In 1980 I went to West Sussex'80 with another Canadian Guider and eight girls. This was an International Boy Scout/Girl Guide Camp for 2800. From these two International Camps I was able to cobble together a vision for my own International Camp, SERENDIPITY '83. [450 Guides and Guiders from 9 countries]. I have no idea how many Guiders worked hard to make it a SUCCESS. Pat Drugge, Kate Schurer, Ann Junkin, Irene Hurford, Sally Gibbeson, Babette Brown and many, many more.

My youngest daughter, Marcia, who was 17 died of a brain tumor in 1981. What a shock. We had no idea until about ten days before when she went to an eye doctor who spotted the tumor, sent us to a neurologist immediately. He booked a CT scan, an angiogram and there was no time to think only follow the procedure and ask God to please do what was best for her. I didn't want her to live so we could watch her suffer but save her if she would have a decent life. Yes, I said that prayer over and over. She came out of the operation and anesthesia and seemed fine. She could wiggle her toes and all but when I said I thought she would make it. She said, "Really"? She knew much more than I did.

By the time George got there I had phoned everyone assuring them that she looked good only to go in with him to find her tongue curled up and her need for intensive care. Losing someone you love at seventeen is stunning. I phoned my cousin a nursing instructor in California after they told me her kidneys had failed. Sarah asked if I knew what that meant—I did. The priest gave her last rites. The social worker talked to us briefly. Being unfamiliar with death and not knowing what to do I decided we all needed whatever sleep we could get so we left. We returned at eight the next morning I went in told her we'd miss her, that maybe when it was our time she'd be there to guide us. I said Good Bye and sent George in. five minutes later she was gone.

I had run for town council in 1980 missing by a few votes. In 1981 I stayed home to look after my family after Marcia died. I ran for council again in 1982 and was near the top of the poll. I resigned in time for a replacement to be voted in in 1983. Our marriage was disintegrating.

In January 1984 I went to Japan to stay with Motoko, a Japanese Girl Scout leader, while I sorted myself out. I learned some conversational Japanese in 1983 and began studying to complete my B.Ed. I was almost finished it when I accepted the job of Program Director at the World Association of Girl Guides and Girl Scouts Center--OUR CABANA, in Cuernavaca, Morelos, Mexico. I started after Christmas 1985 just after the earthquake in October that created havoc in Mexico City. I learned a lot of Spanish and management skills. And left with many new friends scattered all over the world ZIPPING ALONG takes over from here. Enjoy.

UNCLE BERT, KELLY, AUNTIE CATHY, KORI, RANDY AND YVETTE.

Chapter one persons of interest
Me, Zip - 47, 5 foot 2, eyes of blue....
Fran-my friend since Grade Thirteen. Omer, her husband
Mary the coordinator of the Therapeutic work programs for CMHA
Ray, the woodshop coordinator
Sal one of the employees in the coffee shop
George, my ex-husband Ona and Joan
Yvette my dark haired brown eyed daughter, mother of 13 month old Randi
Nancy, my red headed, blue eyed daughter taking her Architecture degree at UBC
Susie, my middle sister, who managed a KAL tire shop

CHAPTER ONE

COMING HOME

"Well stranger, welcome home". Fran gave me a big hug. Fran and Omer were at the airport to meet the Mexicana flight I'd taken from Mexico City. They heaped the luggage with all my treasures collected in the past two years into the trunk of their car and we headed to North Delta.

"You can stay with us until you get settled. How's Nancy?" My daughter, Nancy had been living in my suite looking after the house while I was away. Nancy was studying Architecture at UBC.

"She's writing exams and working part time at Community Sports. She moved near UBC a few weeks ago so my place is empty. At least I have that. I'll need a car. Without one how can I find a job or get to visit my friends and relatives?"

"Okay Zip I can help; how much can you afford?" Omer asked.

"Not more than $3000. I'd prefer a Japanese make if possible."

It was snowing and it looked like it might stay. I'd have to dig out the clothes I'd left behind. I'd have to see Nancy to get the keys. Paul, my godson, had had the new gutters installed, so that was great. Nancy had put in double glazed windows, so there was way more light in the basement suite, and she had installed plush carpets in the bedroom and living room. The only incomplete project was the set of concrete retaining walls needed so a garage could be built. Nancy had drawn up the plans, found an engineer to approve them, and a contractor to put them in. Soon they were in place as well as the foundation for the garage.

"I found two possible sets of wheels. Omer said. Let's go check them out." I took along my cheque book. We had the small Honda insured, and on the road the same day.

Now I could settle into 7797 Elford. Over the holidays Fran, my sisters and old friends kept me busy. I had a lot of catching up to do. And, I found a job working for the Canadian Mental Health Association.

"Welcome. I'm sure you will manage the Therapeutic cafeteria program well. It is a big responsibility-purchasing the groceries, assigning the staff, and keeping the menu popular with the customers," said Mary.

"I'll do my best." We provided coffee, tea, cookies, muffins and light lunches for anyone at Lucas Centre. Nothing too fancy. The staff included people with schizophrenic tendencies, a few battling bipolar symptoms, one mentally challenged individual, and one fellow who couldn't cope with crowds.--about fourteen people, some men, some women, of varying levels of skill and reliability. Mostly they were amiable, happy to have a job, something to do with their time, and to earn some spending money. A few of them had fried their brains doing drugs. One day the cookies or muffins would be perfect, the next you might have to throw out the whole batch.

A couple of days stand out in my memory—the day I learned that one young lady who had babysat a lot the month before had gone to the welfare office, reported her meager earnings, and lost most of it because I hadn't been there to coach her on what she could keep, and what she needed to report. Another day Sal was upsetting everyone. She was slamming cupboard doors, muttering at the others who soon came to me saying "you have to do something"." I'm afraid."

"What is the problem Sal? I asked.

"You shouldn't have slammed my head into the cupboard..."Sal said.

"I'd never do that." "You need to go home." "Please put your apron in your locker."

Then I went to my supervisor and asked, "Please phone for Sal's social worker to come and get her." The rest of the staff breathed a sigh of relief once she was gone.

Then there was the day when Ray came in looking like his world was falling apart. Ray coordinated the wood working program for the Canadian Mental Health Association [CMHA]. I sat with Ray, who had full blown Tourette's. His conversations were usually full of swear words he couldn't control.

"I used a rental agency to help me find a place to stay in North Vancouver. With Tourette's I'd never find a place. They found me a place, so I paid for the first month's rent and the damage deposit—the place is fine, but the landlady seems to be pushing her teen-aged daughter on me. I'm afraid if I stay there I'd be charged with sexual interference with a teen-ager. I just can't stay there; it is too dangerous. I've asked for my money back, but she won't return any."

He had no money, no place to live, and no one to turn to. I explained to our supervisor, then took him home. He slept on the couch until I gave the upstairs tenants their notice and I moved up. Ray was an exemplary tenant. We drove to work together most days. He was dating a young woman who managed a daycare. They married about a year later.

In early March I took a few days off to check out taking a Master's Degree in International Studies in Vermont. In order to be sure my decision was wise, I decided to go there; to check out the program and facilities. Although I had talked this through with my family and friends, I left no contact names or numbers when I flew to Albany, New York from Seattle. I arrived, rented a car; checked into the school in Vermont.

"You should be in class at 9 am tomorrow morning. You can follow the regular program tomorrow. Have supper with us, and get a good night's sleep. See you tomorrow," said the registrar.

I followed the classes until 2pm when I was told "There is an urgent message for you in the office."

I hurried there. "Your sister called earlier [hours earlier]. She is at work but said it is urgent that you call home." I called her.

"George,[my first husband and the father of our girls,] had been killed on the job just out of Pemberton." I was stunned, but my mind clicked in quickly. I phoned the airline, got a compassionate ticket, packed, got in the car, returned to the airport and flew to Seattle to be met by an ashen faced Nancy who had driven to Seattle to pick me up.

Nancy was studying for her final exams in Architecture at UBC. I think she and I were on auto-pilot. This was the second death in our family of five.

Yvette flew in from Portage la Prairie, Manitoba with thirteen-month old Randi. Randi helped us get through it all. We walked under the cherry blossoms in Stanley Park. We had no family portraits, so we had some taken. We dealt with George's new wife, Joan, the funeral, the lawyers and yes, I got a copy of the autopsy results. Tough reading.

Ona made sure she got all the family keepsakes she wanted. She asked for the treasured, large, framed photo of her mother taken when she was about three that had hung over Yvette's bed as long as she lived at home as well as the coal oil lamps, the depression glass—whatever.

Yvette asked Joan for her Dad's Mexican tooled suitcase, Joan sent it to the Thrift Store. She asked for the dining room suite. Joan sold it to a neighbour. She asked for her Dad's pay stubs—He had kept everyone since he began work. Yvette got those.

Because George hadn't written a new will after he married, his old will leaving Yvette as executor was null and void. For her 100 day [approximately] marriage Joan did well. She hired the same lawyer George had used for the divorce. She got the first $65,000 plus one third of the estate. I checked with the IWA to see if she could get the $450 per month pension the union insured workers for, but George had died 25 days short of his 55th birthday, so he didn't qualify. She got the Canada Pension Death Benefit. For fairness, we asked the accountant to be the administrator of the estate. As I had inherited the $30,000 life insurance policy I needed a lawyer. Yvette and Nancy needed a lawyer as did Joan. I believe we were all glad to see the end of it.

George's death shook us all. I did what I could to deal with the necessary documents. I had been planning to go to WS 88 [West Sussex 1988 Girl Gide/Boy Scout Jamboree] in England. I would stay with Betty and Charlie Millins who had hosted me in 1990 and catch up with other friends I had made. However George's death really unsettled me so I decided to take more time, to not waste the cost of the air flight, to wander through Europe as I had never been there; to catch up with Ina [in Denmark] who had worked with me in Mexico, and to try to see Hulta, a very efficient Finnish Guide leader. I needed time to settle myself before I got to Betty and Charlie Millins' and the camp. Hopefully I might figure out what I could do next and maybe to just be. Life was sure to give me a push one way or the other, eventually.

In July I resigned from the Therapeutic Work Program; packed my backpack and headed off to explore Europe. I wanted to see how the Laplander's live, to see what it is like north of the Arctic Circle, to take in the sights wherever I went and learn all I could. As always I was collecting new friends and storing life's experiences.

JAN, INA AND I top;   NIKOLAJ, ROXSANE AND AMANDA bottom

Chapter two persons of interest
Ina a beautiful Danish young woman who had been on my staff at Our
Cabana for 6mos.
Jan, her naval officer fiancé.

CHAPTER TWO

JOURNAL CATCHING
UP WITH INA

I arrived in Frankfurt via Wardair at 4:45 pm. In the airport I validated my Eurailpass,- then took a train to the central station, and got on the train to Hamburg with a second or two to spare. I slept on and off en route. The Conductor explained track 8 for Copenhagen when I changed trains in Hamburg. I met Mary Hilland, who had been on a walking tour of Switzerland. We chatted for most of the two hours between trains. Then she was off to her reserved sleeper and I was off to 1st class. There I met Sharon and soon after, Linus. We collapsed the seats; made ourselves at home and yattered for a short time before Sharon dozed off. Linus and I discussed philosophy and life in general until after we had been loaded on the ferry at Putgarten and unloaded at Rodby. The wait for our engine seemed interminable, and Linus had to make a connection in Copenhagen for Stockholm.

I slept peacefully right into Copenhagen station. There I phoned Ina who came to meet Sharon and I. We went to her home, met Jan, had breakfast, and went on a walking tour with Ina. First through the park to the harbour, then along to Nyhavn with its beautiful boats, the House of Parliament, the Queen's Palace, the Marble Church, the Stock Exchange and into the sailor's church, where Ina was to be married early in the Fall. We had lunch at a Lebanese cafe paying 35K for tuna filled pita bread. We went through the Danish Design Centre, and the Berings and Groendal China Store where we admired the storybook settings designed by various ambassadors' wives. We admired the setting for the Little Mermaid the most.

We window-shopped through many walking areas of Copenhagen, took Sharon to make a phone call, took the train back, bought a tent, went through the food market and through a park called the King's Park, saw the Round Tower and went home for supper before Sharon and I explored Tivoli. In Tivoli, Sharon and I checked out the sights. As there were no concerts on Monday night, we admired the overall layout and the flower gardens edged with beautiful Cleome. Later we stopped for a drink and as darkness fell, the lights came on, turning Tivoli into a true fairyland which we explored again. We returned home for a good night's sleep. The next day we breakfasted and started out a little later going to the Stone Age village at Lijre, it was quite an experience.

You can pay to holiday there grinding your own flour, wearing scratchy-looking homespun garments held on by leather thongs or cords. Ina had prepared a picnic lunch which we enjoyed before heading back to see the church at Ros where Danish Royalty are buried. We checked out the ladies' shops there hoping to find a suitable dress for Ina to wear to a wedding July 9th. No luck, so we took the train back to Norreport where we found the dress, and then enjoyed tea and a pastry. Sharon bought her towel, too. I was only missing my notebook. We returned home for supper, phoned a friend, and got organized for our trips.

We got up at 5:30am the next day, had breakfast, took our packs and headed to Velje where we visited Legoland. After Legoland, where I had an amazing shrimp salad for lunch, we went to meet Ina's brother, Gert. Then we caught a bus to town and met the train to Fredrikshavn by running for all we were worth. We passed through the Danish countryside and arrived three hours later with plenty of time for the ferry to Oslo. There was no discount for us, and it barely passed inspection. We ended up passing the night on the carpeted floor near a table in what was a bar or cocktail lounge. I, of course, fell asleep easily but was awakened by a fight between a drunken couple that seemed to go on forever. After what seemed like half an hour I was back asleep. I awoke once or twice, but all in all I got a good night's sleep. Ina didn't. She had not slept well, and was ashamed of the couple arguing.

I breakfasted on Ryking, peanut butter, and a container of milk I bought the night before. Put our luggage in a locker, and changed money to Norwegian funds to do us the day. We got some tourist info, stopped at a cafe for tea then headed out for the Vigeland Sculpture Park by tram. This we both enjoyed. Then we were off by bus to the Viking Ship Museum and the Folk Museum. We didn't leave there till after 4pm. At 6pm we toured the National Gallery with its Monets, Van Gogh's Self Portrait, and the best of Scandinavian Artists. Then we went for asparagus soup and tea at Samsons. As we still had time to pass, we moved down to observe the street scene which included a Peruvian band playing their haunting music, and later a political demonstration against police brutality and high rents. Later we shopped for cheese, bread and yogurt for breakfast for Stockholm.

We boarded the couchette car which had two young couples as well, and slept from Oslo to Stockholm. Maybe they were going to the Bruce Springsteen concert that weekend or to the Jazz Festival. On arrival Ina and I changed some money, phoned the hostel, and got us space on the Chapman, a sailing vessel built in 1883. We went out, paid, stored our packs, had a most welcome hot shower and did our laundry. Then we ate breakfast on the grass under the trees and planned our day. First to the Swedish Design Center, second to see the display on various aspects of Swedish Life, third to City Hall by which time it was lunch hour.

Ina bought shoes. We had lunch there for 39SK. I had Duchess potatoes, codfish au gratin, a roll, a lettuce and tomato salad, tea and ginger cookies. Too bad it wasn't open Saturday when we returned. The City Hall is famous for its French cuisine. It is responsible for preparing Nobel dinners. We headed out to explore the Old Town which is full of fascinating boutiques and the King's Palace. I bought the candle holder 29K. We headed back for the shop and a nap before supper. We walked back into town looking for a place to eat and finally decided on a nightclub called "Downtown". We each had non-alcoholic banana coolers to drink. I ordered a pasta of the day for Ina and an American hamburger for me. It took about one and a half hours before it finally arrived. This was too long! Meanwhile the waiter apologized and said our meal would be free. We didn't have to worry about what to do with the evening, the food was good, and we just paid for the drinks.

We wandered back and had tea in the park, and then wandered around the islet where the Modern dance museum and an art school are located. We took pictures of the boat against the evening sky. We checked the laundry, set the alarm and made our beds with pellon-like paper sheets. They'll do till we get home.

We rose early, we checked out, and left for the station to wait for Jan. His train was delayed, so we had a light breakfast, changed money and tried to phone Hulta in Finland, but no luck! After Jan arrived we stored our luggage, then went off to the park for tea and Jan's breakfast. The Salvation Army set up and began a band concert while we were there. We saw a different group of them singing in a shopping center an hour later.

We went to the Swedish tourist information and learned where the nearest extensive toy store as well as a grocery store were. Even though we weren't leaving till 6:43 we had to buy our necessities early as the stores all close at 1:30 or 2pm. After checking at the tourist info we headed back to City Hall for lunch...but it was closed! Then we went to Old Town and searched for a place finally settling on one that offered a beer, roast reindeer with potatoes and gravy and lingonberry sauce for 75SK. I decided to splurge, and it was good.

We went back to do some serious window--shopping. And purchased 5 more postcards for 5K and a Swedish print doily for 39K. Later I found a strangely beautiful piece of abalone shell for 15K for Nancy. Mostly the tempting things had been too expensive. Then we headed back to town where we found a MacDonald's for supper [1 fish fillet 14 and 1 chocolate sundae 6.50.]

We headed for the station where I changed some Swedish money into Finnish. We picked up our gear, boarded the train, wrote and read a bit, and napped in between. We shared our compartment with a father and his two daughters, eleven and ten. At 9:30 Rail crew members came to set up the beds. I went out to stretch for a while, but soon we were all sleeping soundly with the window wide open. Someone did get up and shut it when it got cold in the middle of the night. I didn't wake up until almost 7 and then just turned over and dosed some more.

I finally got up around 8, we all dressed and the family got off at the stop before Boden. We left at Boden, put our gear on the grass, and I left Ina to reorganize hers and Jan's while Jan and I searched for tourist information. We found it near a beautiful lake. The girl was very helpful, and spoke English well. We went back to Ina, used the restroom at the station to refresh ourselves, had a tea and yogurt (chocolate Truffle - yum) and got on the train heading to Narwich at 12:40. We met several Americans on a rail tour of Scandinavia- all unhappy with their overly rich diet.

We knew in advance where we'd cross the Arctic Circle so we were all lined up at the windows to snap its photo (marked white stones) Crazy aren't we? The train went slow, and blew its whistle twice. The thick, small forest scenery got boring, and the train's motion put me to sleep. We had pumpernickel bread with cheese and salami for lunch, an apple for dessert, and something like Sprite to drink.

For the second time on a train journey, there was a flood from one of the toilets... washing the floor of our car thoroughly. Thank goodness my luggage was up, and not on the ground.

With the windows open, fluffy bits of seed were floating through. Out the window I could see motorhomes, travel vehicles and campers. The glaciers were getting closer and closer. Earlier I had seen many snowmobiles near homes outside of Kiruna a large iron mining city.

We got off at Abisko- stopped for a sandwich then put our packs on after refilling the water and headed off into the wilderness. It was chilly so I vowed to put on the proper clothing layers in the morning. We walked for about an hour- saw a lovely cascade of water, found pit toilets, a picnic table and a fire pit. One tent was set up below this area. We put our packs down and continued as we didn't believe this was the campsite. However we finally turned back after deciding campsite or not we'd set up the tent, cook supper and stay the night. Droppings proved a reindeer had been there shortly before us.

Jan was feeling cold, ill and lost his lunch. Ina made freeze-dried curried rice for supper. That 5 minute stuff wasn't even properly cooked after half an hour. We enjoyed it but Jan barely touched his. We had lemon tea to wash it down, washed the dishes, reorganized the things and I crawled into bed to keep warm. I used my clothes for morning as a pillow. I remembered to take my anti-histamines (onions in the curry).

I woke up two or three times that night- it was pouring rain, and our neighbours were packing up to catch an early train.

I started dressing about eight, but we weren't moving until about 9. Then Jan made porridge (oatmeal) with raisins for breakfast and brewed some herb tea. Now he was hungry. We washed up, took down the tent, repacked and after much discussion decided to give up on the 8km hike to a former Lappish religious site (offering), and just head for the train so that I could move on to Finland, and Jan and Ina could find their way to the top of a hill where they might see the midnight sun. I decided I'd probably be asleep every midnight, sun or no sun. (I can sleep almost anywhere, anytime, as Ina said right through the barroom brawl ten feet from where I lay, even though I heard her shout at them two or three times to smarten up, treat each other properly, or whatever. She was so glad I couldn't understand what they said.)

When we arrived at the station it was shortly after 11. I'd missed the first train, so we set off to explore a Sami Lap home site nearby. This was obviously part of a National Park display, well maintained, but interesting to explore. We came back to the station, and decided to check out the boutique BUTIK where I found charming Lapp dolls for 35SK each. I bought a boy and a girl, and a postcard.

Jan said we should check out Abisko town proper so we did. I bought an apple there. We headed back and found the next train went to Narvi Norway, not Boden Sweden, so we rested a bit then Ina and Jan made mashed potatoes and fruit soup for lunch. I ran across to the Youth Hostel to use their toilet. What a beautiful complex it is, a cafeteria, lounge, quiet room, all immaculate. The displays and tapestries were fascinating too.

Ina and Jan had repacked, and were ready to hike when I returned. Short goodbyes, then they were off and my train arrived on time. At sixish in Kiruna I was hungry again so I ate the last of the salami and 4 Ryking. We seemed held up on a siding in Kiruna forever. I missed the company that Ina, Jan and a few Americans taking a rail tour of Scandinavia had provided on the journey to Abisko. It was boring, so I started to read Emile by Rousseau. I met this charming ten year old travelling with her grandmother. We exchanged candies. First, my hard fruitdrops, later her chocolate coated caramel bars, DAJM, both excellent, and our addresses.

I got off in Boden and they continued to Lulea. The train into Boden was about two and half hours late so there was nowhere for Max Hendricks to have supper. I decided to share some RyKing and peanut butter with him. He's an Aussie, finished his degree in accounting and economics, and is now almost through his law degree. We both stayed at the Standard Hotel, I in the hostel type accommodation, and he in a single room. Earlier I'd met Harry Reiger of 4600 block Fourth near Tolmie in Vancouver, an older gentleman full of life, who was running short of cash as he'd expected to put his costs on his credit cards. He had travelled a lot, enjoyed soccer, World Fairs, etc., had raised two daughters and obviously enjoyed the company of both Lorraine and Karla.

In the morning after a breakfast of muesli, yogurt, RyKing, salami and cheese we all headed for Kemi via Haparanda. The train to Haparanda was only ten minutes late. On it we met a red-headed, chubby Finnish lady who kept us up to date on travel info, prices, etc. She knew that the train connecting Haparanda and Kemi had been replaced by a bus, but that the Eurail pass covered the bus cost. In our 2 ¼ hour layover in Haparanda, Max and I walked into Toron, took a couple of pictures, and had an early lunch at a beautifully decorated salmon coloured fast food place. There the daily special was a heap of mashed potatoes covered with eight meatballs, lots of gravy and lingonberry sauce with salad, and whatever one chose to drink for 28S- an excellent buy, and very filling.

We returned in time to exchange information with Harry and await the bus. On the bus each of us chose a seat near the front of the bus, and an Iranian traveller from England with a Danish passport chose to sit with me. We really couldn't converse well. At Kemi, the train station waiting room was elegantly done in Art Deco style with shades of grey turquoise and peach. The washrooms cost 1 FM, about 35cents, but were immaculate. The train ride from Kemi to Rovaniemi brought Sally Miller, an Aussie working in England. Max and Harry had continued to Oulu.

Sally and I passed the trip talking to a Japanese fellow who had a year off teaching to do biological research in Finland. From Rovaniemi he was taking a bus to the North Pole. Sally and I got some tourist info in English, and checked into the hostel 37 FM. We ended up in the same room. She showered, and I did laundry having left my towel in Boden. Later we went for supper at the Kantakrouvi on Kansankatu #8. She had minced reindeer, and I had the baked Finnish cheese with cloudberry sauce and tea for 30 FM. The place was a bar complete with modern music, and full of mainly young people. It was dark inside, so quite a shock to come outside at 9:30 to broad daylight. I took a photo of a building with a flowing roof, then came in to get Hulta's phone number and try to reach her again. I got a new number after several tries after asking the girl at the Youth Hostel desk for help. Then I continued to try getting busy signals until 10:30 when I gave up.

The next morning Sally and I got up, and shared the litre of milk we'd bought, rushed to store our gear at the train station, and catch the 8:45 bus to Santa's village. Whew! We made it. En route we saw a huge jack rabbit- I'd never seen one so large. Santa's Village could stand a lot of improvement. We checked out the cafeteria, post office, decor, and then the small boutiques. We discovered everything was too expensive. Finally we found a place where you could buy the wooden components for mobiles or Christmas ornaments, so we each bought a few. Then after checking out the designer shops and all, we bought several postcards only to find the next shop had several better ones. So we bought them too.

Both of us were fascinated by a shop called Moskitos which used the pesky insect as a design on knitwear and suspenders very effectively. There was a quality jewelry store where the ptarmigan pendants had a white side for winter, and a grey brown stone for summer- an interesting practical feature making them more adaptable.

We then went for a cup of tea so we could write our post cards and mail them from Santa's Village. We also wrote down a couple of addresses so Santa would mail personal letters to our tiny friends. I found a delicatessen that sold hard tack wafers and packages of sliced smoked reindeer meat, so we bought some for lunch along with some soft cheese this we enjoyed at the bus stop just before returning to Rovaniemi.

In between times, however, we visited Santa's workshop to see their displays especially those pertaining to Christmas around the world. The animation was very simple, and in general there had been little or no research into the different ways Christmas is celebrated- definitely not worth the admission price in spite of the slide presentation on local flora and fauna- this again lacked professionalism. We left to find the reasonably priced gift shop that a Dutch girl we met had been excited about located in the parking lot. First we found a place with gorgeous sweater sets, fur hats, and air brush and stencil designs. Again, we looked- it was pricey.

Then we arrived at the bargain souvenir warehouse stores and some items were indeed better buys. We both debated a couple of items: Sally, a wooden heart, tiny bird serviette holder and I, a knit ear-warmer that said 'Polar Circle'. We headed for the glass shop, where we each purchased something; Sally, a five inch plate with a Summer Lapland scene painted on it, and I, five embossed glass Christmas ornaments. We both left satisfied with our choices, and enjoying an ice-cream cone.

By the time we got back we had to look for the bus stop to head to town. On the way back I spotted a reindeer. In town we got off at "City Market" a large supermarket department store where I replaced the towel I'd left in Boden, found 24 colour print film for $5 a roll, and bought apples for our evening meal en route to Oulu. We then headed for the tourist info to inquire how to say 'Cheese' in Finnish as well as where we might be able to buy a book in English to read. A book in the bookstore (Penguin paperback) was over $10, so I decided to continue with 'Emile' and Sally to do without.

We caught the train to Oulu and I slept at least half the way. In Oulu I tried phoning Hulta again but no luck. I enquired at information, and they gave me her address and bus directions, so I decided to store my gear in a locker say goodbye to Sally who was off to a youth hostel, and continue my search for Hulta. The mosquitoes and black flies at the bus station were terrible!

I caught the bus, and got off at the indicated spot with another woman who told me she lived in the building next to my Friend, and would help me find her. We found the apartment, but the name had changed. I rang the bell anyway. The red head who answered had trouble because I spoke English, but she told us Hulta now lived in Luxembourg and for her address I could either contact her parents (she gave me their address), or KOP the head office in Helsinki could probably give me her address too. I chose the latter having given up on foreign phones for the time being.

Outi took me home to her apartment, phoned a friend, made tea and Kareilian cakes, Danish pastries and peaches. Every time I suggested leaving, they assured me I had missed the early train and would only have to wait in the station alone for the 20 past midnight train. Outi looks like a younger model for the painting American Gothic… flawless skin, severely or simply styled reddish hair, and that special look in her eyes. We discussed many things. She is a music teacher, her father is a sea pilot who loves history, and keenly researches it advising historians when he finds errors in their work. She is a strong believer in God, a Lutheran, her friend said as are 90% of her countrymen. However, not so many are as secure in their faith as she is.

We later discussed how to teach cooperation, multiculturalism, and peace building skills. Her friend drove me to the train station after we located his car that he forgot he had left at the supermarket. We found it when we went to phone a taxi after deciding that we had missed the bus. First he thought his wife might have taken the car as it wasn't where he usually parked it. It was confusing. He was obviously even more absent minded than I am. We got to the station, checked to see which line the train came on, got my pack from the locker, and he left.

I got to the right line, and boarded the train for Helsinki as soon as it arrived. There were no first class seats, but second class was very nice even though I couldn't get to sleep until about 2am. It was still broad daylight. About this time, just as I was about to doze off I discovered that the cap had come off my mosquito repellent, and it was leaking all over the contents of the front pocket of my pack. I had to throw out some chewing gum, a plastic spoon, and a few other tiny things. The plastic cover of my lipstick felt terrible too. Oh well, now, every time I open the pack I check the lid.

I slept- awakening about 6:30am in time for a sponge bath in the train washroom before arriving in Helsinki. By the time we reached Helsinki I'd decided to purchase a Helsinki card. Take the half hour city tour, and jam in as much as possible after leaving my gear in a locker at the Silja line ready to board for Stockholm. I took the tram out and back as far as market square where I bought a box of strawberries which served as breakfast as I quickly gobbled them up while exploring other stalls. Things were cheaper there. I loved the fur hats, and decided to buy a reindeer skin for Nancy for her birthday. Then I just had to pack it with me for the rest of my journey.

On the way to the city tour I came upon Fazer's, the famous sweet shop where I bought a chocolate 'truffles' ice cream cone for 8.5FM. I thoroughly enjoyed it. What a breakfast. When I arrived at the tour place I thought there wasn't going to be enough room, but they squeezed four of us on at the last minute. Our tour was given in English and German, and the guide never got time to catch her breath. We saw Senate square crowned by the Cathedral, and got off to take a few photos. Later we stopped at the Sibelius monument and the Church on the rock, which is spectacular. The tour was informative, and saved a lot of energy after a poor night's sleep.

On our return I went to Stockman's to see their Finnish design display, and to collect my free gift -5 postcards. From there,I went to the Finnish National Bank to get Hulta's address in Luxembourg, and from there to Saplanade- a wooden design shop, a glass design shop the Palace cafe for lunch- a huge bowl of pea soup, flat bread, cucumber salad, butter tea and 3 scoops of ice cream for dessert (pear, nougat and chocolate) all for 28FM. A healthy, filling meal. After eating, I went in search of the Finnish design centre, found the name on a building, enquired, and was told that it was on the other side… it wasn't. I checked further along the street I'd been given- gave up and went to the Museum of Applied Art instead. There was an exhibition of Irish Design, as well as a fairly thorough collection of Finnish Design. Some pieces by Alvar Aalto were outstanding- I remember especially a piece of blue glass. Also, a carefully designed three legged stool in birch and leather was outstanding. The photo exhibit of nude people in happy positive attitudes was in sharp contrast to the exhibit in the next room showing war and war related developments.

While at the Applied Arts Centre I ran into a Zontian group of women who were having a conference in Helsinki. They believe the development of women is the development of the world. After the museum I made a quick tour of the tree lined boulevard Esplanadi street where I picked up a copy of Finnair's "Blue Wings" and went into a Finnish couturier shop where prices began at 2500 FM for a jacket made of a highly textured fabric available in many colours and black trimmed with satin and diamond, or triangular accents,to add life and contrast. A group of French women were looking for "a smaller size in the same colour" and trying on style after style. Next I went to the Marimekko shop. The fabrics she designs are so pleasing to the eye- there was a little of everything, including toddlers' clothing and household linen. Time was flying, and I was weary, so I headed for the Silja line and checked in about five minutes before the ship was opened for loading.

I soon found myself with new acquaintances, a couple from New Zealand (retired) who were over for 51 days. They'd enjoyed Scandinavia but found prices high. They told of being mugged in Spain, but some locals returned the bag with contacts intact as they had intercepted a would-be robber who was breaking into their locked sleeping compartment. We settled our gear in, and then made for the upper deck (9 floors) to see the islands and the city fade away as we left port. It was beautiful, so serene, and the temperature just right.

A comic touch was added by a training vessel for young seamen. It was so small in comparison, it seemed like a toy and we joked about the sailors going home for dinner. Back inside we checked out the prices in the various restaurants then I went in, and had a welcome shower with plenty of hot water. I never did venture below to have the sauna I'd planned on. I slept for an hour waking a little hungry, so I returned to the cafeteria for cheese to go with my flat bread, hot chocolate and yogurt that would hold me till morning. I went back below, and moved into the sleep-in section provided. I settled in, and slept until about 6:15am. I got dressed, worked on my journal, caught up with my New Zealanders, and then went up for a breakfast of cheese, Ryking, hot water and yogurt.

I went onto the sun deck to see the islands as we approached Stockholm. Later, waiting to get off the ship I met a Brazilian woman, Zela, 56, who was travelling around Europe with her 12 year old daughter Eli. We were to be companions for about 24 hours. Zela had been robbed on a train in Italy. They had taken all her cash except for 18 lire as well as all her jewels and unmounted stones that she had brought in case they ran out of money. Now she was sleeping poorly due to the stress, and not eating well in order to feed her daughter. We got into Stockholm together, saying goodbye to the New Zealanders en route. We discussed our plans for the day, then decided to put our luggage into lockers, and leave together on the 10:48 train to Kobenhavn –sleeping en route. We went downstairs so we could purchase milk and bread for their breakfast (half l shared and two sweet rolls) for me, I chose 2 bananas and some yogurt, keeping one banana for later in the day. Over breakfast we decided to take the tour of the interior of the City Hall, and to see the Wasa Museum. We agreed that walking was best for all of us.

We arrived at City Hall with twenty minutes remaining before the next tour started, so I went to get information on how to get to the Wasa- about a forty minute walk. The tour began in the Blue Room, which isn't blue at all. Apparently before it was painted the architect came through and saw that the red brick in the natural light had a special life of its own, so he had its surface carved and decided against having the blue added. However, due to previous advertising it has retained its name. The steps are designed for ladies with long dresses to descend graciously.

The city administration chambers have a beautifully decorated ceiling typical of Viking halls with lighting placed to give added emphasis. The red ochres, sea blues, and accent colours are so typically Swedish. The Gold Hall where Nobel banquets and presentations take place is a fabulous work of art. Gold mosaic provided a perfect backdrop for mosaic works done in the best Italian tradition to provide a progression of some highlights of Swedish history.

As the tour concluded the pert, pleasant Guide told us that due to budget overruns they had no money for a roof, so anyone who could afford to do so donated _____KM per copper roof tile and had their name recorded in an account book that is carefully stored. The names of course began with the King and Queen of Sweden.

After this tour we began to walk our way along the harbour towards the Wasa. I could see that both Zela and Eli were tired. Sleepless night,s and a poor diet showed. Finally I suggested we stop for an ice cream-Zela agreed, but wanted a drink instead. She and Eli shared a Club Soda, and I had trouble drinking my whole 7-Up but they refused my offer to share. Refreshed and somewhat rested, we headed off to the Wasa, noting the buildings, the water, and other scenery en route. Earlier we had passed the soldiers heading for the changing of the guard under mounted police escort.

The Wasa was on an island just past the Nordic museum. Here we rested a few minutes before seeing an English presentation prior to our tour. Again the Guide, a lively Swedish miss, did an excellent job of explaining the preservation process, the restoration, the reasons for the sinking and the reason why the Wasa was so poorly designed. The Swedish king wanted his boat to be bigger than the one just built by the king of Denmark, so he had an extra floor added making her too heavy. If they added enough ballast to stabilize her or water would enter through the gun placements. Luckily, the Wasa has been reclaimed from the sea and has contributed to our understanding of mankind. (Don't be greedy or overly proud.) After our tour I found a washroom, then Eli and Zela wanted to rest in the shade a few minutes. We found some grass in a park under a tree and stretched out.

Twenty minutes later we were beginning our search for a McDonald's so Eli could have a big Mac. Along the way they found a package of shackles that Eli will take back to her Dad. We stopped to get directions to McD's as I was sure there would be more than one and the one I knew of was quite far. Along the way another couple gave us different directions, so we followed a well known safety procedure asking person number 3 who confirmed #1's directions cluing us into the easiest way. McD's provided its standard fare. Eli had a Big Mac, and shared fries ands a drink of a Coke with her Mom. I had a 6-pack of McNuggets with mustard sauce, and a chocolate sundae. I offered to share with Zela, but no! Later they accepted some peanuts.

We left to do the shopping they wanted to do. We entered NK Stockholm's largest department store, set a time of forty minutes and agreed to meet again at the same spot. I went to see the 'The Very

Swedish Store', a portion featuring quality souvenirs and exclusive Swedish Design. I browsed, idea shopping as usual. Later I went up to see the latest in ladies' and children's wear. At some point I spent some time in their kitchen ware section- I like their style. Returning through the grocery section I tried the elevator along with another couple from New Zealand. This only led to various levels of the carpark so with the aid of a Swedish family we returned to the grocery section and found a stairway up. I got to the main floor with five minutes to spare but I couldn't find the meeting spot. I went out the nearest street exit, and walked around outside until I found the entrance I needed. Zela and Eli arrived about five minutes late, having bought a tiny circlet of silk roses to use with a candle for the Virgin Mary. We went on down the street, glancing at stores right and left until we came to another large department store where they wanted to shop again. This time twenty minutes only as we still planned to get to Uppsala before we left for Copenhagen.

I took a chair and people watched till they emerged with the Swedish crest Eli wanted to give to her friend. Now straight to the station. There was a train to Uppsala at 19:05- it took about fifty minutes travel, we could stay about 1 hour and then catch the 21:05 train back to Stockholm. Off we went resting en route. At Uppsala I caught sight of the castle tower and headed us in that direction. We found ourselves on a path that had a cross trail going almost straight up. I enquired and they agreed. We headed up, and soon there were ten people following us. The castle was beautiful,and now serves as a social sciences centre for the university. We headed to the Cathedral next; what a magnificent creation, but sadly we had arrived thirty minutes after it closed. We made our way back into town crossing the stream, and continuing through the older quaint section to the shopping district as I wasn't quite sure of the shortest route to the station. I asked some young ladies who said we could follow them as they were headed in that direction. We got to the station in plenty of time, and headed back to Stockholm.

I checked to see how many coins I had, and gave them to Zela to put with hers to buy something as they'd have no more value outside of Sweden. Eli bought a litre of milk for us to share. We drank part before collecting our gear, and getting into a compartment on the train for Copenhagen. There was a Japanese fellow in there who was most dismayed to see us arrive as his hopes of a good night's sleep vanished. He went to look for a better spot, but finding none returned. Strangely enough, this same man was almost crying when I left the train two stops before Copenhagen.

Yes, I'd been using my Spanish to communicate with Zela all day-listening to her Portuguese, Spanish or French, and replying in Spanish or through Eli who spoke English and translated our needs as required. Now I dug out my Japanese phrases from the dusty corners of my mind and began to learn about this man who has some kind of business in Italy that has to do with teaching math. His family, a wife and two daughters, would meet him in Madrid at the end of the month. As we talked about Japan and his family, he must have become homesick for he called his family from the ferry. Eli and Zela wanted advice on which types of videos to buy, so he tried his best to sort out the information they required . He must have gone to sleep and dreamed the answer for it was the first thing he wanted to talk about when he woke up.

We were told to get off the ferry on foot as we had boarded it in Helsingfors, and now watched as the train we should catch left the station without us. Someone said there'd be another in five minutes at 6:03, but that train didn't run Saturday or Sunday. Next we thought there'd be one at 6:14, but I went back to check and this too didn't run on Saturday. The one we wanted left from track 4 at 6:25, so we all loaded our gear and got to track 4 in time. I was informed there was no first class on this inter-city train. We all spaced ourselves hoping to get a little more rest. Eli at least succeeded, as she was still asleep when I left the train. We all asked God to look after each other. I headed for the steep stairs, and the train pulled out.

I found my way through the station, and travelled the few blocks to Ina's. I opened the front door with the key she'd lent me, and knocked on the door, Jan opened it. They were surprised to see me so early. They were getting dressed to go to the wedding, and had to leave by 7:40 am, so I sat down to talk to them during their preparation. After they left I washed all my clothes, and hung them to dry. Then I had the second half of my breakfast, having eaten a yogurt, some flat bread, and cheese on the ferry. We finished up the milk at that time, too. Here I had some pumpernickel bread with sausage (salami?) and tea followed by more bread with black currant jam. I became tired so curled up for a short nap before going to buy the paper to mail my parcels home. I got up, made a box from some cardboard I found, and managed to fit in the Lapp dolls the Christmas ornaments (glass and wooden) the candleholder, the table centre, the bear baby toys, and some papers I was keeping. I inadvertently put in two films I'd taken so I hoped they wouldn't be x-rayed. I went to the store, got three sheets of paper, and I came back to wrap things as quickly as possible. The reindeer hide was awkward. I added a jacket, a jumpsuit, and some papers to it. I lugged these to the station in Copenhagen and took a number at the post office. When it was my turn I was dismayed to learn that it would cost $15 each to mail them. but I decided to go ahead. The small packet they would take but they wouldn't accept the largest one unless I paid more than double and sent it by air and so I ended up carrying that package all day. I realized due to the cost of postage I'd need to cash more money (change my Swedish and one 50 Swiss Fr cheque#12] again I found myself in a line up and waiting. Solved that, and went to reserve a seat on the train for Koln leaving Sunday at 9:15pm. I took a number. 367 it was, and they were looking after person 309. Needless to say I was there a long time, long after all the other post offices would be shut, so...I had to bring the parcel back to Ina's, and en route I bought some groceries as all those shops were closing, too. I found a place a few blocks from the station, and bought some potatoes, apples, nectarines, pumpernickel bread, and yogurt.

I came to Ina's took my clothes in as it was going to rain and they were almost dry. I sorted my pack. Had a short nap, made a supper of potatoes and eggs with a nectarine for dessert. I read Eurail info and Youth hostel info trying to come up with a better plan. At 8:30pm I turned in for the night. I awoke at 7:15 really relaxed. At 7:45 I had breakfast a yogurt, bread, and cheese. Later I had a shower and washed the clothes I wore yesterday. I hung them to dry, put my sleeping bag out to air and began to search for handcraft books to copy patterns from. This I did, alternating with writing my journal and looking for the iron. At lunch-time I shredded some potatoes and cooked them up with a little sausage for flavour. I ate, packed my sunshine-aired sleeping bag and my pack. Finally I located the iron, ironed my shirt, and two pairs of slacks. I got everything, even the sleeping bag, into the pack. I washed up the dishes and tidied up.

Then I began reading "Lost in the Cosmos" a book I bought in Stockholm. Ina and Jan arrived, Jan feeling much better. The wedding had been simple and quiet, ideal for the couple. Jan began making supper, Ina and I talked Guiding, Mexico and crafts. Supper was beef (rare) and a potato and cucumber salad with a yogurt curry dressing-very good. Ina made me a variety of sandwiches for on the train..

I tried placing calls to Uta and Hulta and Thor's friend- no luck. At the station I tried calling Nancy, then Yvette, finally got Allen to tell him I was OK,, and ask how everyone was. Yvette has another cold but was off to the Strawberry Festival with Randi. Went out to the platform, found the car, and the seat, then out to say a moving farewell to Ina. Who knows how soon we'll meet again, and we mean so much to each other.

There will come a day
When we can't be near each other
Because of this you have to know
That you always will be part of me
Your thoughts, your actions, your words
Everything you gave me is in me
Maybe there will com a day
When I'll forget to write
But I'll think in anyway
We'll always be a part of each other
The time we had nobody can take away
I'll share you with others
But never give you away.
Merry Christmas
Hope to see you all sometime, Yours Ina

Chapter three persons s of interest

Hulta {really Helena] a Finnish young woman who had come to Our Cabana for the Juliette Lowe session representing her country. She came back leading a group of Scouts. Dan, straight from the kibbutz, he was my companion from Koln to Koblenz and more

CHAPTER THREE

FINDING HULTA

On the train I am with three Persian people who have been in the US for eight years. The boy has just finished high school, and will go to a Junior College to study Business Administration followed by more at UCLA or Cal State. His mother and aunt are very dependent on him and his English. His sister finally got out of Iran eight months ago, and is living in Vienna, learning German quickly, and hoping her husband can join her soon. They were so happy to see her again. She is studying English, too. The aunt is tired, petulant, wants to sleep but not across as is most comfortable. She has her own sheet and pillow, so for her maybe it doesn't matter. 1. She doesn't sleep for long 2. She can't find her Railpass when the conductor comes, so at 2:45 he stands there forever with all the lights on while she fumbles eventually telling him, "You come back, I look and find it, OK?" and the light stays on another twenty minutes. Finally I shut it off. She is spoilt, used to being cared for, unaware of others' needs. They check tickets at least three times during the night as well as early morning. David and his mother slept in the next compartment, probably glad of one night without the bother of the Aunt.

In Cologne, I left the train, headed for the information desk to find out when the next cruise down the Rhine covered by the Eurail pass began- it was twenty to eight, and she said the boat was three minutes away to my left outside the station, and left at 9am. I hurried out, happy with the news and suddenly found myself face to face with the most impressive Cathedral I've seen- what a work of art! How much time spent to make this tribute to God, and how sad that these same people probably didn't see the suffering of mankind, or was the Cathedral like a giant public works program leaving behind something that lifts one's spirit, and inspires us? There are so many possibles, aren't there? I slipped in, admired the structure, the amazing intricate stained glass windows, indeed the absolute power and the glory. Right next door is the Roman Germanic Museum, a modern architectural work. What a contrast. I saw a few large paintings and displays- one showing 'plastic' type American people who worship 'the now', and a war display showing its pointlessness and horror. I took a picture of the two architectural forms, and then proceeded to find the boat information, and ticket centre where I purchased a river guide for 5M.

We boarded and I found myself on the sundeck with a blue canvas chair, in the company of three Americans- a couple from San Diego and a young chap from Chicago who was returning home via Europe after having spent ten months in Israel, working as a volunteer and studying. We travelled down the Rhine in varying degrees of sun ranging from a slow broil to solid overcast. We noted the churches, Beethoven's Opera house, the residence of the president, and many industrial sites for oil, coal, ore loading, and barge loading. There was usually a cycle path and park area along the banks, often, barges passed us and at times we passed trailer parks jammed with trailers 2.5 feet, or less apart- worse than an apartment holiday. There were castles, monasteries and vineyards. At 11am we went down for lunch- I had parsleyed potatoes, red cabbage and sausage for 960 and a pot of tea for 5M (exorbitant!) . for a total of 15M was about $12. Occasionally the captain would announce items of interest on either shore, and occasionally German music would float through the loudspeaker. This was a wonderful lazy introduction to Germany. We stopped here and there to take on, and unload passengers in a smooth operation. Most of the German women on board wore skirts and attractive blouses, and very sensible sandals. They were definitely a conservative group.

We noted that the barges often were family homes. The wife was up in the wheelhouse, and the window curtains were lacy, ornaments or potted plants lined the window sills. Some villages resembled the quaint towns on a model railway set. Vineyards proudly displayed their names in white. Forberg, Rosenberg, Weinort, and Leutesdof. In some places the steep hillsides were terraced. At Andernach we saw an 180' high tower from Middle Ages, and a 400 year old crane for loading ships. In many places the trees lining the shore hid the buildings we wanted to see, and made photographs useless. Also at Andernach a white swan floated gracefully by. We passed a large Portland cement plant but by this point our numbers had thinned, and the crew began to fold up the deck chairs and tidy up. A nuclear power plant and bridge under construction loomed into view (Neuwied) 1300 megawatts RWE we were told, but it seemed to be in full operation.

After getting off the train in Koblenz, we asked for the next train to Mainz. It was 6:51, but an InterCity, which meant that Dan would need to pay a supplement, so we waited for the local train at 7:02. I suggested this as from the Inter-city we wouldn't see the castles or vineyards as well. We changed some money. Then when we found the right track and knew we had time, Dan ran back to buy me a drink, and himself a chocolate bar. We settled in to a simple 2nd class no smoking car. However we were soon joined by a group of young men travelling together from England (or so it seemed.) They were very high (excited), and were generally behaving poorly. I was very pleased to see them leave at Boppard in search of the hostel. I really didn't want to pass the evening with them. We kept watching for castles, then Dan said he didn't know how to tell a vineyard so I explained. We both felt this part of the Rhine was very special, and that this was where we should have taken the boat cruise. (Mudener Funkenberg vineyard on the Moselle).

After sitting on a few sidings while the express trains whizzed by we arrived at Mainz, located the bus stop and met a very helpful young man who explained which bus to catch, which stop to get off at and where to buy the cheapest bus tickets. He was riding the same bus and continued to act as our guardian angel as we didn't understand the stops as the conductor called them. We got off the bus at the right stop, and attempted to follow the young man's directions but ended up asking 8-10 people before we found someone who knew where the carefully hidden youth hostel was. We arrived to find a note on the door saying the hostel was full. We went in to see what they recommended, and the fellow began to say they were full -then he took a look at me, and said he had a bed for me and a second or two later, one for Dan. We quickly paid our 16.50DM, ordered cereal for breakfast, and left to find our rooms.

I proceeded down a dark hallway, found the room, and couldn't decide which of two beds was in use. There was a shower and sinks with the room that slept 6. Toilets were down the hall. I rearranged my valuables, and went off to find what facilities the hostel had, and what the rules were. I met "Bizzy and Heather" from Vermont who said shower anytime, breakfast in that room, and suggested we go get a drink. 0.80M yielded a small hot chocolate, very hot. By this time Dan arrived and asked if there was anywhere we could get supper or even a chocolate bar. No luck and the hostel curfew prevented a journey back to town. We decided to turn in, and to check with each other at breakfast. I tried for a shower after talking to one of the girls from my room who said they'd be up late as they wanted to talk to the reception fellow after he got off work. The shower ran, but I could only get cold water so I decided on a sponge bath by the sinks. At least I felt refreshed. I rinsed out my underwear, and hung that with my towel to dry, made my bed and crawled in for a good night's sleep. I awoke at 9am got up, dressed, packed and went for breakfast. The cereal turned out to be a mixture of muesli, cornflakes, and raisin bran served with ½ l of milk and a fresh pear. A great way to start the day.

Dan arrived. He'd decided to head for Wurmz and I into Mainz to make the calls to Hulta and Nancy and to buy the doll parts I wanted. Happily I managed both. Hulta was very happy, and very surprised that the phone call was really for her, and that I had tracked her down. I arranged to phone her when I arrived in Luxembourg and to see her in the evening. Nancy was getting ready for bed. She and Eric were showing his parents the town. She had a soccer game coming up. Ceci and Isa will arrive from Mexico the 25th of July and stay until Aug 3rd, so I'll just miss them. Happy with my 16.2M phone calls I left in search of the doll parts.

I got directions from several people, and took a bus as I was carrying my pack. The store was easy to find but the first three clerks found it difficult to help me so they sent for Claudia who found all the doll pieces I needed. Even though it cost 104DM I was happy to have them. Mission accomplished, I went out into the market square, took a couple of pictures of the DOM (cathedral), but couldn't find the entrance way to see the windows. Time was flying,so I bought two bananas in the market, and left to catch an IC train for Koblenz.

The four German ladies in my compartment were very sociable. One had a humorous book with her: the other an Agatha Christie mystery. The others had brought along buttermilk with dark bread and cheese sandwiches for a late breakfast. I ate my pear from the youth hostel. We checked out the castles en route. I was interested in their story of the Lorelei, a siren who sang so well that she lured a young boatman to his death, and of the Mat and Mouse castles belonging to two brothers who fought. We arrived in Koblenz.

I deboarded, and caught the train down the Moselle to Trier. This was again beautiful scenery, with vineyards climbing the steep hillsides, and at times lining the valley floor. I enjoyed the company of two Norwegian girls. Ana and Katerina who were also going to spend the night at the youth hostel in Luxembourg. We all got off in Trier. I wanted to see as much of the city as I could in the four or five hours I had. I put my luggage in a locker, asked directions for Porta Nigra and was off, after a luncheon of three potato pancakes (oops I forgot the onions) requiring two Tums for the onions,and the calcium. Then I spotted Florentines in a bakery window,so I had one with tea in a bakerie, along with an anti-histamine, of course. Then I walked along to the Porta Nigra, took a few pictures, checked with information, bought a map, and headed towards the centre of town, the market square, and from there to the house of Karl Marx.

There were several contrasting architectural styles and many fascinating shops. I went into a toy store to admire the dolls, and did see dolls like the ones I make for about 500DM. I found a nicely illustrated child's story book about a small angel with a tiny gold nose. It is all in German, but I bought it anyways. I headed on to Karl Marx's home, toured the building and watched a video. Thinking I must get several of his works to read. I headed back, stopping to take a photo of the statue in a square, and then to buy a small piece of embroidered braid to use, maybe even on a dress for Randi.

Suddenly I realized the time and headed quickly for the train station, buying another cup of tea and a piece of cheesecake at the same bakerie as before I'd been given an extra cup of hot water for free. The servers were very pleasant. Here I bought a tin of cold Sprite to use up my German coins, and after buying some sugar coated peanuts at the station I still had a few very small coins left. I got on the train for Luxembourg and watched as the vineyards gave way to dairy farms, and the dairy farms to cereal growing. We soon arrived in Luxembourg where I joined the queue for changing money. There I met two young fellows- one from Scotland (Mohammed Ali) and one from Australia, Brett. We went to the youth hostel together.

I used my French several times before we reached the hostel. After I checked in, and sorted my things I phoned Hulta and arranged to meet her an hour and a bit later at Place des Armes- the focal point of Luxembourg. In the time I had, I decided to eat the rest of my lunch, shower and wash my things out before hiking into town. I was twenty-five minutes early so settled myself to enjoy the folk dance presentation in process.

Hulta arrived at the information booth and we were pleased to see each other. We caught up on simple news, checked on our mutual acquaintances, listened to the orchestra that took over from the folk dancers, then changed tables to order 'tarte a la maison' and hot chocolate. As the waiter said the dessert was yesterday's. We found it neither tasty, nor fresh but with the aid of a little whipped cream we survived it. Besides, I had been rather hungry. This was the first wheat I'd had knowingly had.

We talked about many things: Guiding, our lives, when our Mexican friends would arrive, what we planned to do the following evening with them, and what I might do the next day. As I didn't have to meet the group until 6pm at the hostel, I decided to go to Strasbourg in France- feeling that two or three hours would be better than not getting to France at all. At 10:30 we parted. I walked back to the Youth Hostel and Helena [Hulta's real name] went to her boyfriend's parents' home where she lives while she has her summer job at the bank. I checked the timetable and found I needed to be at the station early which meant preparing my breakfast, brushing my teeth and crawling into bed. Of course, I'd taken all the things I wouldn't need out of my daypack so it would be lighter. I slept well, awaking on time, gathering my things and walking quickly to the station.

I went early in case there was an earlier train. No such luck so I ate my breakfast while I waited. I also changed another 50 SF into money for Luxembourg. I was concerned about not having French money, but hadn't thought to ask for my money divided half and half. I got on the train and found myself sharing the compartment with a medical student from Holland. She was black, so was afraid of customs problems in France. She was good company, so the time to Strasbourg passed quickly. After arriving I changed 500 Belgian francs into French francs so I could have money for a drink- I was terribly thirsty and needed money for museum entrances. I had a problem locating the tourist information, but when I did, I discovered that that the Art Gallery I'd come to see- was closed for renovations. Then I asked about the Cathedral, and finally asked for her suggestions. I purchased a map and headed off following her directions to the canal lined section known as La Petit France- a picture book area of quaint homes with an aged grace that brought them to life beside the canals. I passed many expensive restaurants, and eventually found a grocery where I bought a tin of apple cider and one of 7Up. I drank these, ate my crackers, cheese and a meatball I'd purchased in Luxembourg along with an apple.

I visited the St Thomas church, a lovely old Lutheran church where an organist was playing calming, delightful music. I made a donation in hopes that the church will be preserved, and remain a pleasant sanctuary. It seemed a very special place to me. I spent two hours wandering past the closed shops, and galleries only managing to buy four postcards. I headed back to catch the 2:41 train to Luxembourg, and realized I had some French coins to get rid of. Because of this I went to an outdoor cafe near the station where three scoops of ice cream cost me about $5 in coins, a horrendous price, but keeping the coins which were worthless elsewhere would have been stupid. The return trip provided me with time for a nap so I'd be refreshed for the arrival of the Mexicans. I changed the French paper money back into Luxembourg currency at the station.

I walked back to the hostel where I surprised the Mexicans after enquiring at the desk where they were. I was pleased to see Pili from

Puebla, but happily surprised to meet Karin Knape from Mexico City along with the rest. Karin and I had a lot to talk about. Diana was going to be in Finland, too- I'd miss her by a few days- too bad. We talked and talked, then got ready to go to dinner with Hulta. We walked to town to a bar called 'Yucatan' it had Oaxacena decor, lousy music but good fruit based drinks. One of the men took a shine to Karin so one of her drinks was free. We heard later the bar was the brainchild of two Americans who didn't want to go home. After about an hour during which we made the acquaintance of Daniel and Cindy, we left, I and the Finnish girls, Maarit and Heidi, walking, and the rest by car, for the pizza parlour Bella Napoli on Strasbourg Street.

Here we had supper. I had Coquilles St Jacques. Most had pizza and a few had pasta. It had been more than eight hours since the Mexicans had eaten, and they were starved. The food was reasonable and well prepared. The waiter arranged for us to tell the cashier what we'd each had and to pay individually. We left, one car making two trips to take us we thought to the hostel, but no, to a pub. Maarit, Heidi and I were both tired and afraid of being locked out of the hostel, so we left a few minutes before 12 thinking maybe we could walk. We headed in the wrong direction so had to return, hop in Daniel's car, and get in by the skin of our teeth.

I went in to find that in spite of my bed having my sheets, and pillowcase and my washcloth, and t-shirt on it, someone had moved in. Her friend went to advise her and she quickly moved her things. I crawled into pyjamas, got to bed, and fell asleep. I didn't wake up until after 7am the next morning. By the time I was up and dressed, there was only half an hour for the Mexicans and Finnish to make it to breakfast. They did, but Mimo had to go back up for the tickets for the group breakfast. I had my own breakfast, but ate in the common room and managed to get some tea. We'd all discussed what to do until we met Jim at the tourist information at the Place des Armes at 2pm. Shopping, window and otherwise, was the order of the day. Maarit and Heidi were looking for shoes. Pilar wanted to buy cheap but good watches. We decided to try Scout House first.It was drizzly. We found an elderly gentleman who said something about 3 in the afternoon. I remembered something Helena had said and decided it would be from 12-3pm.

We went into town, dispersing to check out the items we wanted. The scarf I'd admired the day before turned out to be 3750 francs- over $100- not within my price range. We checked shoes, watches, etc and finally Karin and Erendida bought Rambo-type knives. They thought these would be great for the camp in Sweden. We went up to Place des Armes taking photos and checking along the way. I bought some bottled water and a chocolate bar. Then rather than lunch we headed for Scout House again. We met Helena and her friend heading for lunch. Yes, we were in the right place (near her bank.] The man met us again, and said no, not now, from 3-7pm. We headed back to Place Des Armes to hear the end of a school band concert. We went to MacDonald's for lunch, a filet of fish, hot chocolate and fries. Later after surviving a downpour by taking shelter in the bandstand. I went down and bought an apple and pear for the next day. At one of the shoe shops I found a large scarf for 200BF- a good buy. I bought one. This along with the green leather purse I'd bought before going to Strasbourg the day before,were my major purchases in Luxembourg.

At 2pm we met Jim who took us on a walking tour of Luxembourg. First he took us through the casements, an ancient underground fortification made in stages by the French, the Spanish and others. They used to control the river so they could dam it and flood the enemy if required. At first we walked down 129 stairs in the stairwell area carved out of sandstone- it was by no means moisture proof so some areas were a little slippery. We saw the placements for the small ship-sized cannons and one larger cannon on display there that was to be removed as the dampness was ruining it. These passages are kept locked as people have become lost in them and put in a cold night. At one time the casements were considered as a shelter from a nuclear attack but as they weren't leakproof the idea was discarded. We went right to the bottom of the gorge to see the sluicegate.

We later walked back through the park that forms the valley floor. We also saw the cathedral, the Ducal Palace, and the rest of the ancient ruins and connecting casements at Urn Bock. In the distance one could see the EEC center on the hillside designed by Teillard de Chardin who also designed Montreal's Olympic Stadium. The people stopped it from being completed After our tour including the suburbs, Jim left us at the information centre. From there we again headed for the Scout Shop where belts, banners and crests were purchased. Now it was time for home- to meet Hulta at 6pm. We stopped for fries and a hot dog for Karin and Monica, and I got some chocolate ice cream. We got back to the hostel, dead tired,but I put on my Guide top, Monica and Karin changed, and we headed off minus Mimo and Felipe who hadn't returned. Helena left all kinds of messages for them, but we met them half way back into town.

We went to the American café bar "Interview" where we met Daniel and Cindy again. This time we waited for them to finish their coffees and piled into their cars to go to the "Fontanella" another Italian restaurant. We mostly ordered pasta this time, and no one had space for dessert. The food and ambience were both much better than the night before, which had been reasonably good. The staff and variety of the food were pluses. Our little United Nations was fun. Pili, Karin, Elendira, Monica and myself wanted to go straight back to the hostel after as we were beat. I said goodbye to Helena (wish I'd met her boyfriend Yves) we must keep in touch. How lucky I've been to have Ina and Helena here.

I organized my things, set my alarm, and said goodbye to Karin, Monica, Pili and Erendira then slept like a baby until 6:30. I dressed, finished packing, ate a simple breakfast and waited to check out at 7am. Then I headed straight for the station as quickly as I could go. Just as I got through the door something behind me snapped and I could feel my pack pull to one side, but wanting to attend to first things first I went in to check which track number and the precise time of departure. There'd been a change since they'd printed the schedule. The train now left at 8:31 not 7:55- Whew! I could relax. I left my pack sitting, and went to check when the stores opened as I wanted to buy another scarf, but no luck. The 8:30 opening would be too chancy.

CHAPTER FOUR

ON THE ROAD AGAIN

I got on the train and shared a compartment with a stiff, proper older woman. I slept on and off to Namur, but noticed the country was used partly for grain, sugar beets and dairying. I got off in Namur, put my luggage in a locker got directions to see the citadel, an immense construction from Roman times. I took several photos, and had the tourist information person explain the underground fortifications, a few singular buildings and the area where I might find handcrafted articles or/and craft supplies. I found a few interesting shops as I was dodging the rain, which would pour on occasion. Finally I found a shop with weaving and silk painting supplies. I bought a silk painting book.

Then after checking out the sales and the clothing designs, I went to the Crepe Bretonne for lunch. I ordered a cheese crepe followed by one with rhubarb sauce- an excellent lunch with a glass of red currant extract and soda water. The restaurant was cozy, dark, and warm. The lights were draped with squares of lace that added a little to the atmosphere. I left warm, relaxed and with the decision to skip Brussels as it was pouring, and I wanted to settle into the youth hostel in Bruges. As I got off the train in Bruges, I met two Australian nurses, and two Californians who had decided to go to the Bauhaus hostel. They phoned, and were told there was room, so we hopped on bus #6. A friendly gentleman told us the right station.

The girl behind the counter assigned us our rooms. She placed the young women who had come with me, and two Italian young women all in room 10, and me in room 8. I went back after talking to them all to see if I could move from #8 to #10 but was assured the other beds were full. I knew my room had two males there, but that was no problem for me. However it apparently was for Gabrielle, a French art teacher who was in the other bed. She really needed another female in the room to feel safe. I went out with the ladies from rm10 to get a feel for the town. After walking to the Administrative Palace and the Town Hall, three of us decided to go back and have supper. On my return I met Gabrielle, so we talked a little and she agreed to come with me and have some tea or coffee while I had supper- a salad followed by a Dame Blanche (chocolate sundae- vanilla ice cream and whip cream) combined with hot water was just right for supper. After some edifying conversation on French habits re: gossip, etc, I decided to turn in early so I'd be able to see a lot before leaving for Oostende the next day.

Gabrielle decided to wash her t-shirts, blouse and slacks- they were all white. Since she couldn't find a place to hang her clothes she spread the wet ones on an empty bed- when I looked in the morning the mattress and all were soaked and her clothes not very dry but she decided to wear them anyhow. Brrr! I'd had my shower, packed and she still showed no sign of being ready for breakfast or to go to the market early as we'd discussed the night before. I went down for breakfast- a bun, two slices of bread, a hard boiled egg and jam- I got Lisa to save my place, take my bread and bun then went up to get my Rye wafers. I told Gabrielle I'd be leaving in about 15 minutes. Lisa and I became acquainted over breakfast. We decided to wash up and in five minutes leave to explore the town. We were off by about 9am. Lisa knew where several things were located- the best money exchange place, the travel agent, etc. So I changed money, bought my ticket to Dover, and asked the travel agent where the market was. She directed us to another square. However when we arrived we found this to be a market of food and clothing for local people with little to tempt tourists.

We set off again following Lisa's book's directions. We found the Church of Our Lady, and went inside where we found the Madonna and Child carved in white marble by Michelangelo when he was only 24 years old. The marble was polished like satin – a serene, loving work showing the amazing talent Michelangelo possessed. We left a donation for the maintenance and preservation of the church. We continued down the street, past many interesting shops, priced the canal boat tour, explored the deguinage where women who wanted to remain single, but not become nuns, had their own tiny homes. We were looking everywhere for a market that sold lace. We went in one shop to ask but the sales lady was busy making a good sale to a French woman. After some time I decided to try farther along. We decided to buy some Belgian chocolate. I finished my 100g on the train to Edinburgh. They certainly were delicious.

The shopkeeper told us there was no lace market, but that there were a couple of old ladies down the narrow street opposite that might sell us some lace and that there was a flea market on the canal banks but that it would be poor due to the cool rainy weather. We didn't find the ladies, just a tiny chapel surrounded with cottages with lace bobbins in the windows. Maybe we should have knocked on the doors. We turned back to find Walpin Square, another lace market possibility, and the Lake of Love. We returned after being redirected to the church courtyard. We took pictures from every angle, and even though we tried to wait until our shots would be pure architecture, usually someone would get into the picture frame just as we went to snap the photo. It was frustrating.

I went into the museum to ask where this lace market was. The fellow told me there probably wasn't one; that I might be able to buy some at the school; but that most lace sold in Bruges was made in Sri Lanka or Indonesia. We went out, turned right and wandered through the flea market. The only things reassembling lace were a few maltreated doilies, both crocheted and knitted lace. We decided to return, and take the boat trip which was well worth the 110 BF we paid even if we'd already seen the whole tour from the other side (the land side) on foot.

After checking a couple of nearby stores, we began checking restaurants menus for both regional specialities and prices. Lisa wanted mussels, and I wanted chicken waterzooi. We worked our way back to the central square where we found a restaurant that served both at reasonable prices. I chose tourist menu #2 which included cheese fritters, salad, chicken waterzooi with parsley potatoes and chocolate mousse for dessert- we decided the tea was extra. Lisa's cost more as she ordered her salad, mussels and dessert separately. As we finished a couple near us were having Crepes Dame Blanche. We speculated about having this for supper.

After lunch, we shopped, checking each store within a block of the square then we headed for the lace centre Kantcentrum and the school. First we found a store with antique lace displays and lace making supplies. Everything was well displayed. Lisa loved the antique lace, but didn't have the $35,000 to buy the 2 foot table runner. She bought some Christmas beaded trees and I bought two handkerchiefs, one Christmas tree and a baby bassinette to put on a card for Ina later on. Then, looking back we spotted the Kantcentrum which looked closed, but we got in for a quick look around as it was 5pm and closing time.

We went out wondering what else there was to see, and Lisa remembered we were near the windmills so we went out to see them arriving just as they were taking the sails down. Then Lisa wanted to go back to Walpein Square and the Lake of Love. We took a wrong turn, so ended up seeing more country than we would have. Eventually we got to the Square, and found that the gates Lisa wanted through were closed. After trying a few closed doors, and getting through, we were preparing to go over to try the gate when someone else did. It was closed. We took pictures of the canal, and the swans, and then found a restaurant in a beautiful setting that served Crepes Dame Blanche so we both had that and tea for supper.

We headed back for the Bauhaus where I caught up with Gabrielle, and the two young fellows who shared the room. I thanked them for letting me leave my pack there all day. None of us had found any lace anywhere except in the shops. The fellows left, I put my jacket on the floor, stretched out and slept for half to ¾ of an hour. Gabrielle was taking about heading to Amsterdam, then Spain. At 9:30 I left wishing everyone a great holiday. I caught the bus, and chatted with the driver till we reached the station, caught the 10:22 to Oostende where I tried to spend my change but everything was closed and the machines all needed 20F coins. I spent my 5F coins on lemon shaped bubble gum that I gave to some youngster. Oostende was chilly, and dirty, so I got aboard the ferry as soon as possible. I was quite tired, and have no recollection of the ferry. I slept, waking several times before we reached Dover at 6:30am.

CHAPTER FIVE

UNDER BRITISH SKIES

The skies were leaden, and there was a steady drizzle. We filed through to immigration where we stood for about 50 minutes with our packs on as they were understaffed, and many foreigners did not understand the questions asked. It was a frustrating, tiring, experience not made any the easier when one official opened a new gate, and took the end section of the line rather than speeding up the queue by taking people in order. Many people were stewing about making connections for London. I asked an official where I could validate my Britrail Pass, and which track the train ran on. The train fellow said to get my pass validated in Victoria station, and just to ride with the coupon. This got me to London.

I had the pass filled out, and got on the subway. 60p to King's cross and the 10am train to York. I settled in, and dozed fitfully from London to Stevenage and again off and on to York. When I checked in for the train to York I heard the woman who collected the tickets say to the fellow on the platform, "That train's full, you know". How right she was. After walking with my pack and gear through four cars with all seats either taken or reserved I finally found a spare seat at the tail end of the last car, sitting next to a woman who appeared to be studying architecture and across from a very prim and proper friendly lady who was retiring to Straun near Aberdeen. She was a kind, gentle person, very easy to talk to. The woman who was to have been my seat partner decided she didn't want to sit backwards, so she moved to one of the seats that was reserved from York to Edinburgh or Aberdeen.

I was just beginning to understand the system. Too bad many others didn't, as between each car there were clusters of six to eight people and their baggage with no seats. York was great. I bought a map at the tourist information, stored my pack at the left luggage station, and was off to see York Minister, the impressive cathedral that is being maintained, or restored to its original condition. I poked around the outside of a few nearby shops, got my bearings, and headed for the Shambles. What a joy this area is! Tiny crooked streets, or lanes with houses jutting out so the upstairs people could almost reach out the window, and shake hands with their neighbours opposite. It is a quaint maze of specialty shops, boutiques, and eateries alive with tourists of every description.

I was amused to overhear a shop keeper tell a customer he couldn't buy a novelty, a jumping frog unless he bought a postcard- 'Sunday blue laws, you know.' He laughed, and said 'what an expensive postcard" and left to advise his friend that he'd need to buy a postcard, too. In one shop I bought a roll of film, in another a couple of postcards. I was sorely tempted by a navy sweater with green frogs on it- thinking of Nancy, but it was 100% wool so I was unsure. Oh well. I've thought of it often since. I bought an ice cream as I wandered, and later got some lemon shandy and a Cornish pasty for on the train. The wanderings must have tired me out, so I rested and ate my supper.

I got off in Edinburgh, stored my luggage and went with two Japanese girls I'd met to find the University accommodation. It was a healthy walk. They got settled, and we went for supper at an Italian place called Pinoccio's . The chef wouldn't allow me to just have soup, so I had just tea and they had pasta, one with mussels, the other with ham and tomato sauce. Both declared the meal excellent. After the meal we parted. I wandered back to the station to catch the 11:25 to Aberdeen, taking a chance on a few photos as I went. There were many beautiful spots. I did sleep most of the way to Aberdeen although I woke three or four times. Halfway there though, I dug out my sleeping bag to get cosier. At about 4:45 we had to leave the train in Aberdeen. With the advice of a fellow traveller I located the one heading for the Kyle of Lochalsh, and after some time managed to find a fellow who let me aboard where I found a compartment, dug out my sleeping bag, and slept for 1 ½ hours before we left.

About ten minutes before departure, a young Scottish lass who was going to Uni to study "physics" in the Fall joined me. She was working in the Lake District at a restaurant or hotel, and had three days off to spend with her parents on the Isle of Skye. We noted seals on the Ness river, and another woman (well dressed, conservative, white hair, simply done, accepting, slightly plump, calm) who had joined up provided a map with commentary of the journey from Inverness to Kyle. I enjoyed reading it. and watching for the highlights- like a quiet guided tour.

This woman was going to select a new home on the Isle of Skye. Her husband is a chiropodist, and finds the demands of his practice in London too taxing so they've decided to move to a smaller practice. They aren't quite ready to retire, but want less stress. There is another chiropodist near Skye who will welcome exchanging ideas, and be someone to consult with on occasion. It seems like the ideal solution. She was sure she would love the home the agent in Skye had found. In Kyle, I located the tourist info, and enquired about buses to Armadale though there were many things pulling me to Portree. Maybe I should have gone there but, there is no point in stewing- I'll have to see that part next time. On the bus journey to Armadale I shared my seat with a teenager whom I asked if she were given the choice, would she spend the night in Armadale or Mallaig? She said 'Armadale' because 'she was prejudiced', and I told her a prejudiced opinion is what I wanted. I admitted that I maybe should have gone to Portree, but she said the view from Armadale was better as she and her mother left the bus.

At Broadmoor, a seven year old girl and her mother from Vermont got on. They had spent two weeks enjoying the tranquility and warmth of Broadmoor. Tomorrow they'd be in Vermont (mother's voice reminded me of Barbra Streisand; the girl was inquisitive, out going, like a breath of fresh county air. The highlight of her trip had been Windsor Castle. She was also impressed with seeing the seagulls all over a rock in the distance- just like white specks- only to have them fly away changing the landscape. She noted the sheep were the same- white specks on the rocks until you got close to them. I decided to spend the night on Skye. Getting off at Armadale I was surprised to find only the ferry, a cafe and craft shop- no town. I enquired in the craft shop about bed and breakfasts as the place was inviting, but the shop-keeper had no idea, but told me to walk into town, up the road to the crossroad, then left, find the post office on my left, and ask there. This I did though it was a 10-15 minute walk. At the post office the lady told me all the singles she knew of were full, and the fellow I'd overheard saying he was full until Wednesday was the one from the youth hostel. I asked where was the best place in town for a meal, and she wholeheartedly recommended the hotel. I walked over to the hotel pub (11:45am) and was told the menu wouldn't be ready until 12 noon, so I left my pack and took off to get some photos of the wild tree fuchsias, the shoreline and general beauty of the place.

It began to drizzle, so out came my anorak again. I inquired at the hotel on my way back, and found she'd let the last of her singles. She gave me the phone number for a good B&B, but it was likewise full. There was one place left but she assured me she wouldn't send her dog there. She'd been busy typing when I came in, and I didn't realize till later it was the day's menu. She was pleasant, efficient and gracious, a blessing to any establishment. Back in the pub when the menu arrived I chose the potted crab with toast and a lemon meringue with fruit. It was an excellent gourmet choice- the potted crab came with lettuce, tomato, lemon and toast. The lemon meringue was a meringue with lemon juice over it, filled with whipped cream and topped with a fruit salad of bananas, grapes, apples and oranges. Delicious!

As others came to the pub for lunch, two couples ended up next to me, and I inquired for some advice as to where to go and stay. The fellow sitting next to me advised going to Fort William,and taking the bus to Oban. I wandered down to the ferry in plenty of time to check out 'The Ragmuffin's, a delightful little shop full of quality garments mainly combinations of knit and woven woolens carefully designed and assembled. There were also bright cotton fisherman's smocks, well chosen post cards, and a remnant of hand-spun wool.

I proceeded to the ferry, which had a carefully engineered deck section that allowed it to load or unload cars at whatever height the tide or dock set up was. This was possible as a section of the over deck could be lifted or lowered hydraulically. Arriving at Mallaig, I gladly took the train to Fort William as it seemed like all the homes were identical. Mallaig was not at all appealing. At Fort William I went in search of the tourist information where they found me a room to share (B&B) if some other woman came along. It was 9£ for the night, twelve minutes uphill (very steep) but easy to find. I was in the home of the John MacDonalds. I'd been desperate for a bath, but a shower and good night's sleep would have to do. Mrs McD showed me to my room and kindly brought me a cup of clear tea. She sang familiar songs as she went about her work, and had a beautiful white Scotty dog. I began to reorganize my pack getting ready for a bath, a good night's sleep, and early departure the next morning. After a rest, a shower, some writing and a snack, Mrs McD came to check what I'd like for breakfast, and to inquire at what time. She suggested watching TV and turned it on low so I caught the news. Iran and Iraq were settling their war, HURRAH!!

After, while getting cosy in bed, beneath the comforter, I watched two half hour British comedy shows, refreshing entertainment. I slept well, woke a few minutes ahead of my alarm, got organized and went to the dining room for the tasty breakfast of bacon, sausage, egg, tomato and rye crisp bread she had prepared. The marmalade of course, added the finishing touch. The dining room had some excellent paintings on the wall- possibly inspired by Van Gogh, but they were the work of her husband, an excellent colourist. The McDs were genial people- great hosts for my first ever B&B. Mrs McD pointed out the path through the park that took me down the steep hill to the station in jig time.

I got on the train for Glasgow and prepared to enjoy the scenery featuring the heather pushing out between the iron stained rocks, rolling hills later on, surprise gorges with their clear bubbling streams and hills upon hills at times dotted with sheep and sporting Christmas tree farms. The stations were small, often with flower boxes well tended. Several passengers, myself included, rushed to hang out the doorways for photos when Loch Lomond and other memorable scenes came into view. We saw civilization encroaching as we neared the top of the Firth of Clyde, first larger towns, then ship building-the sun was trying to break through the cloud, and our time in Glasgow grew more promising.

I left the train, found the tourist information- bought a map, phoned the Youth Hostel several times but decided it must be their lunch hour, then phoned the YMCA and got a room (6.50£ incl. Breakfast) along with simple directions on how to get there. This was successful . After dumping my pack in the room I paid and received a tour to acquaint me with the facilities. I was given four keys- one for the outside, the front door, the door to my floor section and to my own bedroom. These rooms were simply and adequately equipped, used for students during the university terms. The staff were very pleasant. I quickly organized my things, and caught a bus to town.

I found a maze of shops called Savoy Place. Most of the boutiques were cluttered, and not to my taste, but just as I was giving up and looking for my way out, I came across a sock shop that had the scarves I was looking for 5.99£, better then that 9.99£ I'd seen in London. I bought two, paying by travellers' cheque. I asked directions to a bus stop to take me to the Glasgow Garden Festival, and a fellow customer volunteered to show me the way. She'd lived in Ottawa once for a short time, but had returned to Scotland. The bus journey was over in no time, and I found myself going down and under the bridge to get to the entrance.

I paid my fee, and picked up a brochure on daily events. I noted a fashion show at 3pm, so headed towards the rotunda. There was, of course, a line up, but as soon as the show was ready to start, a gentleman came to place us as quickly as possible. I joined two older women with youthful faces who were obviously enjoying themselves. One was learning about gardening. She was definitely the outdoor type. Their comment was that they were absolutely getting more than their money's worth. The fashion show models were ten young people who had been unemployed. They were trained to work as models for the duration of the show and were doing an excellent job. Most of the clothes featured Scottish woolens used in conservative Scottish manner, but the far-out found its place, too. The large scarves such as I had just purchased were a common feature, as were ruanas in place of top coats. There was a lot of black,and a lot of softer, sadder shades- autumn had arrived.

While I watched the show, I enjoyed a pot of tea, and a slice of cheesecake with black currant toppings. I left to wander through the botanical garden (not as extensive as Lorna's mother's), and a very humid tropical environment featuring orchids, butterflies, all kinds of moss, insects and jungle dwelling plants. The next highlight I enjoyed was the Britoil display featuring an animated robot acting as Hugh Miller, a stonemason that had discovered many fossils of plant life, sea life, and petrified wood. He had questioned many of the beliefs of his day. The whole display was impressive, educational, tastefully and carefully presented! Following that I wandered through several outdoor gardens noting the effective use of flax as a filler.

Strathsclyde College had an excellent presentation showing their use in the community including the areas of research in which they worked. Various cities also had displays. One garden had two fantastic peacocks, part flower bed assemblage and part topiary work, eye-catching and colourful. I wandered though a rose garden, a garden for the handicapped, and a lovely rock garden designed by a Swedish woman. I liked the "secret garden sketches", particularly the one submitted by Twiggy. Along the walkways wherever you went there were usually three or more choices of what to do next. I checked out the peace garden with its silvery willows, and sense of tranquility. I collected pamphlets on Humanism and the Quakers.

The next section was about forests. The logging section used plywood cut-out figures very effectively. Inside there was an audio visual display, teaching the length of time required for a tree to grow, and the events that had taken place historically during a tree's lifetime. Then came a shotcrete badger's burrow complete with sound effects. The whole presentation, including forest look-out tower, was very well done. The tower was a play apparatus including a slide, and down came two boys about twelve, in full kilt regalia and yes, they wore sparkling white underwear! I took a few photos, and headed for the display of housing for the future, a series of condominiums design by LAING for maximum use of minimal space. Most kitchens had fridges we'd consider bar-size, a washer, a front loading spin type, and a dryer, as well as a cook top, oven, and microwave oven. The penthouse even had a Jacuzzi type bath in a rare quadrangle room.

From there I caught the mini-train as I wanted to be in the Four Winds Pavilion at 6:30 to hear the Folk Music while I had supper. These performers were not the quality of the ones in the Rendezvous who had provided an Elvis Rock background while I'd explored nearby gardens. The smoked mackerel with curried rice and raisin salad was a filling savoury meal. From there I went to the Architecture pavilion, simply a PR job, and from there to the Crystal Pavilion. By this point I was too tired to really take in all the displays offered. I left, and eventually caught a bus to the centre of town and the Y.

The next morning's breakfast was two huge mugs of tea (strong: with milk and sugar), and two rolls, marmalade, ham and butter. I left the two rolls for someone else. I caught the train for Carlisle and Oxenholme where I got off to catch one to Windermere. The journey passed through peaceful rolling farmland. It was easy to understand why there had been border wars for control of this land. It is harder to understand why people would fight over most of Northern Scotland. We passed fields separated by dry rock walls, and even sheep sorting areas separated by rock walls. It reminded me of Wordsworth's poem "Michael".

At Oxenholme the connecting train to Windermere had broken down, and I was impressed when ten minutes later we were herded into a new bus, and headed off to Windermere. I was happy as I knew travel in by bus and out by train would provide me with different views. The ride was a short one. I arrived at Windermere- found the tourist info who found me a B&B for 10£ at a place three minutes from the train. I checked in and yes he'd accept a traveller's cheque. He explained his breakfast menu- would I leave a note of my choices by the phone please, indicating the time I'd like it served. I asked for advice on where to go by local bus to see the best scenery and get the feel of the Lake District- he thought a bit and recommended I skip Ambleside and do Grasmere where Wordsworth had lived. Wise advice as Ambleside appeared tourist/commercial from the bus.

His recommendation of lunch at the Grey Owl Pub, however, was not as good. The hamburger was greasy, and did not come as ordered. The serving lady was surly, and although I had my traveller's cheques out to pay when I ordered,the fellow did not say that they didn't accept them. The server was annoyed and curt when I went to pay with them. The 1£ price of the burger rose to 2.20 £ with the chips and I'd asked for a plate to remove the bun, tomato and onions I'm allergic to, even though I'd requested the burger without. All in all it was totally unsatisfactory and to top it off the food stayed with me less than an hour, and a half my body objected strenuously.

Now having to pay cash I didn't have sufficient for the bus trip. The bank was going to charge me 1£ to cash a 10£ cheque- a usurious rate so that was out. The coach lines, of course, wouldn't accept the cheque for fare payment so I had to waste an hour and get the next trip to Grasmere.

I checked with a grocery clerk at Booth's, and yes, they'd cash the cheque if I had my passport, so I went in and purchased yogurt and fruit for my evening meal, as well as candy for the journey as I was running out of the fruit drops we'd bought in Stockholm. I returned the groceries to my room, and caught the next bus, enjoyed the scenery and read the folder on Grasmere. As i got off the bus, I got terrible cramps so looked for a toilet which was close by.

From then on the afternoon was enjoyable. I took the bus driver's suggestions, and tried Sarah Nelson's gingerbread, just one, small piece-remembering something about ginger being good for an upset stomach. It stayed comfortably. I didn't like the photograph type watercolours done by local artists. I was tempted by the many Beatrix Potter books, notepaper, and creations but managed not to buy them. I wandered through a sweet shop, and found some characters made of royal icing on a bubble gum ball that were fascinating, so I bought 5 different ones for nieces and nephews. The price -30p was high, but they were creations, and rare ones. Now to get them home intact.

I went to buy a film, but they were almost 4£ rather than the 2£ I'd paid in York, so decided to go without. I went to Dove Cottage, Wordsworth's old home, and paid 2.80£ for their guided tour and the visit to the museum. It was well worth it. The tour guide was excellent filling in details of their lives, accommodation, possessions, and guests. The rooms were small. The dark stain on the walls of the room that had previously been a pub were used to hide the stains from tobacco, smoke, grease and other ills. The Wordsworths enjoyed simple pleasures. The calling card tray was of wood and cane, not silver as would have befit his station. The bed they used was small as people in those days were shorter. The most fascinating item for me was Wordsworth's passport-something apparently invented in his time. He had stamps from France, and several Italian states. Another interesting bit was that as Poet Laureate of England of England he wrote no official verse. He'd declined the post once as he declared he couldn't be pressed to write. He lived on an inheritance that allowed him to be reasonably independent.

The garden is kept as Wordsworth developed it. The museum had several excellent items, but what I enjoyed most were several readings on tape of some of Wordsworth poetry, a fine addition, carefully spaced through the exhibition. Leaving, I went to the church graveyard to see the headstone of the family. My attention went to large stone monument to a woman who had been a great help to her fellow villagers. How wonderful to be remembered in this way. I then wandered down to the tourist information to see if I'd missed anything hoping to get a special photo typical of the Lake district- I did, and my film wound in.

I went back and caught the return bus to Windermere. I made supper, and read my book until I fell asleep. I was pleased by the Vine's careful attention to detail. The dried flowers, the mini-hotpot to boil your own hot water on a tray with a tea cup and saucer, sugar, non-dairy cream, tea, and coffee packet, all this on a tiny table with a comfortable chair, ideal for journal writing, and sorting travel plans, money spent, or souvenirs. In the morning there was a tiny wooden pig with my breakfast of bacon, sausage, egg, tomato. He had supplied the marmalade requested, and butter for me to put on my Ryking. The bed was comfortable, and the down comforter kept me warm that rainy night. Breakfast arrived promptly at 7:30, so I was through and ready at the station for the 8:20 train to Oxenholme.

The train was packed, with almost every seat reserved but I found a place and settled in next to a Bank Loans officer until we reached Crewe at which time I changed seats to one that was not reserved. I changed trains at Birmingham, and was teased by an older fellow who'd obviously had too much to drink. He advised me to take care to not get robbed or worse. I took the train to Cheltenham Spa glad to leave Birmingham, and was hoping to find Marion's sons' name in the phone book as I'd lost her phone number. I got off the train, and found a phone book, but was unsuccessful, and I couldn't remember the name of his pub. I went a block or so, found a deli that sold Loseley Farms ice cream and went in. I bought myself a hazelnut ice cream and talked to the clerk before I got back on the train headed for Bath hoping to catch Hettie and Wyn. No luck there either, and I couldn't find accommodation for a single person except at an exorbitant rate. I had supper- fish and chips, checked into the railway station, and decided to go to Betty and Charlie Millins at Midhurst via Portsmouth.

Chapter Six persons of interest

Betty Millins and her husband,Charlie who had hosted me when I came to England to attend WS 80 the scout/guide jamboree.

Pam and Charlie Crookes, Cardiff, Wales, a cousin of Betty Millins who hosted us in 1980

Joy Betty Millins' Granddaughter.

CHAPTER SIX

AT ROSETREE COTTAGE WITH BETTY AND CHARLIE

It would be late. I felt embarrassed but decided to go. I phoned Charlie and he said midnight to Haslemere and thereafter to Midhurst was fine. He'd wait up. What joy. Now the train that arrived was factory new and the scenery between Bath and Bradford –on-Avon pleasing. I began to relax again. I was sorry it was so dark, and wet, that I really couldn't see Portsmouth area. Here I changed trains again heading for Haslemere. This train was empty so I searched for the guard to make sure I'd caught the right train. And after ascertaining that and how many stops before Haslemere I could relax. This train carriage seemed like an experimental design with a door for every four seats. The seats were a strongly coloured velour and the four seats nearest the guard's station had been violently slashed in about twenty-five places which although British Rail had mended, they were unable to hide the damage.

The journey was short and I found a taxi easily. I inquired about the cost to Midhurst and we set off. The driver asked if I knew where Rosetree cottage was- no, it had been eight years since I'd been there. He asked his dispatcher and she didn't know either. We drove along looking at the name of each home that appeared but somehow I felt he wasn't paying close enough attention. to the street or to area markers. We ended up straight through to the Petersfield Road so I said "no, not near a pub". "so we'll have to go back" This time I spotted the East Shaw sign and eventually the Woolbeding Farm sign and sure enough we did find Rosetree cottage with its lights on and Charlie waiting.

Charlie was happy to see me, and Betty had managed to trade shifts with someone so would be home 5 hours early. He carried my pack up to the room, and reminded me of the low door way, which is less than five feet and asked if I'd eaten, which I had, but we enjoyed a cup of tea together. Then we turned in. I slept well, waking about 7:30, but as the house was still I read and wrote in my journal. I got up at 8:30 and Charlie soon after. I had cornflakes and a banana for breakfast. Charlie and I talked then waited for Betty to come home. While we waited we watched the hedgehogs in the garden. They are so cute.

It was so good to see her again. We yattered over what I had done, and what I would do for the next few days. As she had tickets to "Major Barbara" at the Chichester Theatre on Saturday evening, I decided to stay for that and leave Sunday morning for Wales to visit Charlie and Pam Crookes for the day, returning Monday morning so I'd be back in time for the Midhurst reception. We had bacon and eggs for lunch, the easiest thing according to Charlie. After lunch Betty and I went in to town to get some groceries. I bought some film- got three for the price of two, and three coupons for 1£ off of a roll of film developing. We went back, phoned Pam in Wales so that was organized after a call back. We caught up on all the news. Later Betty and I went into town after doing the laundry, and bringing half in when it started to sprinkle. This we hung in the kitchen to dry, We picked up Joy, and dropped her off for her bell ringing lessons.

Then we went for supper to a small place called "Pummery's". It was a converted home with a room with a fire, great on cool evenings,, and a converted sun porch where we sat next to the door to the terrace watching the sun umbrellas and chairs getting sprinkled. The manager was not happy with the weather. Our meal of herbed pork chops with red cabbage, potatoes, and French beans was excellent. During the meal we noticed a hand from the kitchen reach out the window to take the required rosemary straight from the bush. Also, just as we were beginning dinner, the fellow in charge of bell ringing came in to tell us they were off to _____ as not enough people had shown up at Midhurst. We were to meet Joy at 9:15pm,so we dawdled over dinner, even deciding to have raspberries and cream for dessert. Around 9pm we left heading for the carpark beside the church. On our way we met

Leslie, the car salesman Betty had approached to find a new, or almost new, car for Betty and Charlie to use, and enjoy during their coming retirement. He discussed possibilities with Betty for a couple of minutes, then we were on our way.

We sat in the car to wait and at 9:45 with no Joy, Betty went over to call Charlie. However this phone only accepted phone cards and she didn't have one. At 10pm I suggested to go to Mary's and use her phone to call Charlie. We did. Joy had been driven there by a taxi driver as they had waited for us in front of the church. Betty picked up Joy's suitcase, and we went home to find Joy very shaken, crying because she was worried she hadn't done the right thing. And because she was worried about her Grandma. The fellows called to make sure all was well. We were.

Saturday morning I started off with a chat with Joy while Betty rounded up the necessary tents and flies. When she went off to take in my films and post my cards, I had a warm bath then we tried to track down a chiropractor or osteopath- no luck. We went back into Midhurst that afternoon, and passed the church which had a canopy over the wall and a huge spray of roses, Madonna lilies and phlox over the gateway. One of the daughters of Lord and Lady Cowdray must have been married. On the way back we stopped so I could take a photo. Inside the church the scent of lilies was overpowering. We had an early dinner, and got ready for the theatre. We went to Chichester along the higher scenic route past the race track, and returned the lower, better lighted way. The Chichester Theatre is being expanded using the hexagon cell as the basic architectural form with glassed in walkways connecting various sections. The theatre is tastefully appointed. That evening there were few if any spare seats for the final performance of G B Shaw's "Major Barbara". It was a performance I thoroughly enjoyed.

The weather remained cool and often wet. We hurried to the car, and home to bed as I needed to be driven to Haslemere at 8am to catch the train for Guildford, Reading and Cardiff. At Guildford they are tearing down the old station where some of the ornate pillars seemed either rotted or rusted and weakened. Here we had to wait as many Gatwick trains pass through, and as the fellow said, "If the Gatwick train and the Reading train both arrive at platform 4 at the same time, someone's feelings just might get hurt." At Reading I had time for a cup of tea served with milk (automatically) so I added a little sugar. I ate my Ry Vitas and peanut butter that I'd packed and looked for a chocolate bar. The main cafeteria area hadn't any, neither had the news vendor although he carried gum and every other type of candy. The smaller coffee spot had them so I got one for the journey. The station at Reading had several modern buildings under construction nearby. There is a ruined castle outside of _____ which gives one the feeling of arriving in a new area.

Charlie was waiting when I got off the train in Cardiff. He drove me home the scenic route, pointing out the city below us. At the door we were met by Pam and Mike, their steel grey sheep dog. We had a cup of tea, caught up on family news then had a ploughman's lunch. Since the weather was unpredictable Charlie had mowed the lawn while Pam and I chatted. He no sooner came in than it poured. Later it cleared again but we decided to tour Cardiff castle rather than to risk a soaking on a walk. Charlie decided with that wise decision he'd drop us off then put in two hours on his computer in his office as he was sure not to be interrupted.

I thought the castle would be a plain ordinary castle, but far from it. We entered,and went to check out the Roman Wall under the newer castle walls. This area had had a new frieze added showing the local Celtic villages at the time the Romans arrived, some intermingling, and a final Roman chariot scene. It was well lighted, and very effective. Next we went toward the Norman keep, but it was closed for restoration. From there we started in to see the collections of the Welsh regiment, but it was time for our tour of the interior.

This was a special treat. The interior was designed by William Burgess, a man with a keen love of animals, a fanciful imagination, and a flare for design. One room had all kinds of birds, one represented all the fables and fairy tales, one featured well known scholars over the ages, some had animals carved in the wood work for example, the nut in a squirrel's mouth was a light switch, as was the berry held by a monkey. He was a stickler for detail, taking great care with colour and proportion. From the harem one could only look out, and the room featured many aspects of Middle Eastern culture. As precise, was the room, complete with a horrible figure above the doorway to scare away the faint of heart. The whole interior was delightful. I'd gladly do this tour several times as, I'm sure I'd see or learn of something new each time.

We walked back to Charlie's office passing a circle of stone, smaller but like Stonehenge. Charlie wasn't quite ready when we got there, so while he finished off we waited. Pam gave me a bit of red tape as a souvenir. Stacks of briefs were tied with red tape. Charlie finished up, and we left driving Pam home to prepare 'tea' while Charlie and I took Mike for an extra walk passing their fairy castle designed by Burgess en route. The view of Cardiff from the top of the hill was expansive. We went back to a supper of roast lamb, with fresh raspberries and thick, thick cream for dessert. By the time we'd washed up and chatted a bit, it was too late for the proposed game of Scrabble. Charlie ordered a cab to get me to the station at 8:30am.

In the morning Pam brought me a cup of tea to drink while I dressed and packed. I had a bowl of cereal as well. Then I stewed and fretted as the cab ordered for 8am didn't show up. Charlie called, the cab was a few blocks away, but didn't arrive until 8:09 and we fought traffic straight to the station. The cabbie complained that 8am wasn't early enough, but I felt if he'd been on time all would have been OK. As it was, I paid him and flew to the correct platform for Reading. There were plenty of seats. I changed trains at Reading for Guildford, and at Guildford phoned to let Betty know I was on my way, but she had already left according to Charlie, and was waiting when I arrived. When we got home we began looking seriously for either a chiropractor or an osteopath as my shoulder was still sore. The only appointment available for the next two days was at 3:20 we discovered at 2:20, so I decided to take it, and be late for the Midhurst reception. I ran to change, Betty advised Jan Robson we'd be late.

We made it to Petersfield just on time, and I went straight in. After taking a short history, and doing a reflex and muscle tone check, he determined that the right deltoid was weakest, and decided on a thorough left shoulder massage, as well as an ultra sound treatment for the left shoulder to solve my problems there. He'd like to have seen me again on Wednesday, but I told him I'd be camping. He advised me to keep my shoulder from getting cold, and to try and always carry a balanced load. He gave me his card and a booklet, and offered to teach Guides or Rangers how to lift and carry and along with the reasons for good posture.

We left, and arrived at Jan Robson's at the end of their tea and in time for their songs and singing games. We'd missed having our photos taken for the local paper, but that wasn't important to me. First we had our cup of tea, and enjoyed the family portraits in the dining room. Then we wandered through the parlour, and out to join the songs, meet the Indian Guides, and the Moores. Gradually people left. We returned and had supper with Charlie. Betty went to get a fly or tent, and I crawled in for a good soak in a hot tub. I decided it was time for an early night, so I read myself to sleep after organizing my pack for camp. Tuesday I washed my hair, tidied the bedroom, had breakfast, and then we went to Midhurst to get some bread for Charlie, my photos, and a few things for camp.

Chapter seven persons of interest
Betty Millins and various Guiding and Scouting camp attendees.

CHAPTER SEVEN

OFF TO CAMP WS 1988

The photos were lovely. Betty got her traveller's cheques, and we bought salmon steaks for lunch (12oz for 3.26£) We collected the equipment from Guide headquarters, and returned home. Charlie and Betty loaded the car. We had lunch, talked a while, and left to meet the bus dropping off the tea chest and tents so Betty could see out the rear of the car. Off we went to camp after filling up with petrol. I dozed along the way. Although the weather was cloudy, windy and cold, the tents went up quickly, and it remained dry. At about 5:45pm I was suddenly hungry,so I made myself some peanut butter and RyVita to eat along with a pear and a small banana. Then I learned we should have come with a packed lunch, the result of poor communication. Later Betty and I shared more RyVita, and peanut butter, and at about 7:30 the site Guiders decided to have supper- canned hotdogs in cold buns, and some with ketchup. I did appreciate the cup of tea.

We filled up the water containers, had another cup of tea after organizing our tent, and I turned in early. Wednesday we were up, had breakfast of porridge, sausages, and eggs. We refilled the water, emptied the waste, and I later helped assemble submarine sandwiches of lettuce, cucumber, tomato and ham or cheese which we cut in 5" lengths We overestimated how hungry they were, so we had leftovers for the next day's lunch for those going on out-trips or overnight hikes. We had chocolate mousse for dessert. We all got into uniform, took the cards filled in with name, sub-site, address, etc. and the stamps to trade with other campsites. We had a strip of 6 Chalk Hill Blue ones. We assembled on the sub site at 2:30 (we were fairly late- waiting for the East Indians) then proceeded to the main arena.

After carefully assembling at that point, everyone broke ranks to exchange their stamps. We needed four other colours. We weren't in our groups at all. The opening ceremony was simple and effective. We had a few minutes at the end to exchange stamps, and then we released our balloons on a signal. Some had jumped the gun despite being told we were in Gatwick's flight path, and had to be in unison at the approved time. In the evening, activity cards for the next day were distributed.

Quentin, Freda and I were off to Merrydown Cider makers. Even though I thought Joy Mitchell really wanted to go, she wouldn't take my card, and ended up going bowling instead. Silly woman! I asked if a packed lunch was needed and was told 'yes' but no one said anything to Quentin and Freda until I did at about 9:30. I made my lunch at about 7:30am as we were to leave at 9am. Quentin was reorganizing Ashley to equip him for his overnight on the Southdowns, and he and Freda weren't ready till more or less 9am. It was drizzling, and I was impatiently waiting. When we finally arrived there was no one in line for Merrydown. Quentin said "well, we are the first ones here!" But no! In truth, the bus was already loaded and ready to leave.

Having been on the Sub Camp site in the morning, I met Colin Coventry who wanted to make arrangements for our District to have tea for the Commonwealth chief Commissioner Sir Marc Noble. I went back, told Glynnis, and we told the East Indian girls we'd need them at 4pm as soon as their afternoon activities were over. At lunch Glynnis forgot to get the patrols to each select one member to have tea. I made myself two RyVita peanut butter sandwiches, and took an apple for supper. Then I dressed in my uniform. Glynnis and Pauline prepared the goodies for tea, and got the groundsheets arranged. Fortunately six or seven of the East Indian girls arrived just before the CCC did. We got a couple of the other girls who arrived on site to have tea with us and Jan Jones arrived with two Canadian girls from Bognor Regis.

When he arrived the East Indian girls sang a song pledging themselves to uphold B.P's aims in Hindi. Sir Marc spoke to each of us and then over tea explained that both his father and uncle had been among the well-to-do boys who were part of Baden Powell's Brown

Battersea Island experiment, but neither had become Scouts. He stayed about half an hour, at which time I left for the bus line up for the theatre. I couldn't see Betty anywhere, so I took her camera, purse and money pocket along with me to the bus stop. She'd gone for a hot shower, and didn't turn up until three minutes to 5! By then I was more than slightly concerned. She hadn't packed a lunch either. As we went into London, I noticed Bookmaking shops. We arrived at the theatre at about 6:15 so we had time to wander along the Strand before the performance. We found a drugstore where Betty bought a couple of granola bars to take the place of her supper. I bought some just to have on hand in case, besides, I needed to cash a traveller's cheque. Next we found a Tie Rack shop with a scarf I liked on display so I bought two different ones for 1.99£. Elizabeth decided to buy one to wear over her uniform to change it. She told me she didn't think I could afford the sweater, skirt and coat I liked on display at Savoy and Taylors. It was a "bit pricey," she thought.

Then we got into the theatre and found our seats were the very back row. We were up with the gods. The performance was excellent. I bought us Black Forest Sundaes at half time and tried to explain bits of the plot to the Japanese Girl Scouts beside us. After several rounds of applause we left the theatre, scurrying to be on time for the bus as our driver had curtly told us he could only stand there for five minutes, and he'd leave any latecomers in London. As it happened traffic was thick so he was a good five minutes late, while we were ready and waiting. We dozed most of the way back to camp. I only woke up at the camp gates. Thursday. To Merrydown Cider almost late. Coach already loaded. On our way we were treated to views of beautiful thatched cottages in amongst the brick, stone and Tudor types. Two buses jockeying around a narrow corner, a narrow triangular lot hedged tightly, honeysuckle falling over a cottage door, gardens and greenhouses, a beautiful herd of golden brown dairy cattle, conical roofs on turrets on houses, with strange metal vents from these roofs, B&B here and there, a sign "Carnations- mornings" for sale? I'm inclined to agree with Marion- it's easier to be an eccentric in England. Bush with fallen logo; Woodside Academy offering lessons in hacking, livery and a logged off area, all logs about 8 or 10 feet long, all precisely cut. Enshouse- with two or three greenhouse complexes, then around a few bends and there was the Merrydown Cider Complex however, they were obviously not prepared for us- we'd have to occupy ourselves until the tour at 2pm.

It was 11am, and not a warm day. We went up to see the Farm Museum, but everything appeared closed. While we were wandering around, a young fellow about 9 or 10, came up to tell us that if we'd like some explanations there was a bloke that would show us around. We went and had the milking parlour, past and present, explained to us by an older fellow who resembled John McDougall- tall, gangly-built, barefoot in sandals blue jeans and blue sweatshirt over a blue roll-neck sweater. He had an excellent way about him and a good sense of humour. We were concerned that these people knew nothing of our tour group. They did open the toilets, but we were concerned over the extra costs. I bought a map of the Nature Walk which we might take as I wanted to contribute something. Later Rosemary approached each adult for 1£ to pay the man. I felt this was wise and had exactly that 1£ in my purse. Now I had to rely on my traveller's cheques and my VISA.

We decided we weren't equipped for a muddy hike with some of the English Guiders in dress shoes, and Freda in her sari and I was just plain cold. I suggested we head for a cup of tea in the village. We did, and on arrival at the pub I queried the acceptance of traveller's cheques or VISA. The reply was a definite no on both counts, so Rosemary first and Gay second provided Quentin, Freda and I with tea or coffee. We spent one and a half hours getting acquainted, then I left to find something I could buy to cash my traveller's cheque. The stores had all closed down from 1 to 2 for lunch. The Merrydown shop was open, so I bought a bottle of cider to share with everyone back at camp. The clerk had never dealt with a traveller's cheque before, so I explained it to her. She cashed it. Soon we were off on our tour having been divided into two groups of about 25. The French girl, Laure, asked if the tour would be in English as Nadine didn't understand it. I told her I'd try to help if she didn't understand. The process was carefully explained, and afterwards we saw the movie which added to our information store. Then the other group joined us for the tasting session. The youngsters got generous servings of sparkling apple juice, while we sampled vintage cider. I chose the dry (excellent as were all of the products) elderflower wine, damson wine, and mead. I think the latter would be nice served warm on a cold winter's night. Their products included a range of wine vinegars, special jellies, and mustards. Then we went back to the shop where I purchased pheasant pate, and Gentleman's relish for my father for Christmas. We went out to wait the final half hour before reloading the coach.

On the return journey we again passed through Hayward Heath, a large town with antique shops, a craft shop called Whytchcraft, and the beautiful thatched cottage called Olde Place, for Residents Only. We had passed Piltdown Garage earlier followed by a sign indicating Piltdown Man. I also saw signs telling us that we were not far from the Bluebell Railway, a steam train travelling a few miles. Soon we were back on site. It was cold. We were advised there was a gale warning out, and to secure our tents. I went three times to advise Jan Jones, sub camp director of the foul ups so they could be avoided by future groups. Finally I left the message with the fellow who was responsible in her absence.

I learned I couldn't get the colour of Maxi shirts I'd ordered, so after supper I went to straighten that out, and as it looked like rain to hold seats for the Midhurst group in the bar area for the performance by the folk group "Wilbury Jam". The group included a John Lennon- type bass singer, banjo, mandolin, violin, plying a bass player, and a guitar and oboe playing tenor. They first appeared in tails, later in costumes; the bass player in a suit that reminded me of the British flag, the tenor in golden browns, and a mustard sleeveless shirt and suspenders, and the John Lennon in pin and black striped slacks, a peasant blouse (shirt) and a black shawl. They were very good entertainment. Midhurst arrived late, and were very wet as the storm had arrived. The line for drinks never got short enough so we sat and enjoyed. Then to bed.

On Friday we were off to Covent garden where it appears we were booked into the Transport Museum for 11am. As I'd taken the seat behind the driver, Betty ended up in charge. I'd come away with only two or three photos left on my roll, and forgotten to bring a spare. We passed a goat farm with a llama standing as if in charge of the pasture. Later we got a whiff of cow manure as we passed a dairy of Holstein cows. Further on we spotted a small fruit farm that advertised gooseberries and raspberries and I could see boysenberries as well. We were travelling on H23, a multi lane motorway heading for London. A large truck, carrying racing pigeons passed us. Later in London, signs advertising the Daily Mirror "a newspaper not a comic", bookmaking shops,(betting) (in Streatham??) Streatham Common (park), and a garage for double decker red buses (Alan Ross Sports). The day was lovely and warm. I needed my sunglasses. Chelsea Building Society, Job Centre, Odeon Theatre, WH Smith, Fancy Dress Hire, in an apartment area, "Homan House," Roy Ridley House, "No Ball Games" on a garage, "Workshops" "MOT testing while you wait" "To Let" "Train the Workers Without Jobs to do the Jobs without Workers" "Offices Under Offer" = real estate sign. "British Interplanetary Society" near Waterloo Station Grafitti "Your in a Police State Now" "Sail your car to France for just 45£" on back of double decker bus, past House of Parliament and Westminster Abbey, the Tower, Big Ben, 10 Downing St, House Guards Parade, Nelson's Column and the National Gallery, Watteau to Matisse [borrowed USSR], fancy lampposts in Trafalgar Sq, Mall to Buckingham Palace, Charing Cross Station and the Strand to the Waldorf Hotel where we disembarked for Covent Gardens and the Transport Museum.

We were told to be back at 3pm sharp. We checked into the Transport Museum after passing St Clement's church, and progressing along Drury Lane where "42nd Street" was playing at the Theatre. We saw the old horse drawn buses, trolley cars and such. One car had a movie showing how people used to pass their days off, and another,a movie on women working in factories during WWII, another a video in colour featuring three old time conductors (one a lady) reminiscing about their time on the trams. We climbed up on the double deckers noticing the changes. We stopped to check on the system used to judge sway and up or down motion of the cars, while we ate our packed lunches. We used the 'loo', and left to explore Covent Gardens. The shops hadn't changed a lot since 1980. The seconds woolen goods were more expensive than firsts on the Shambles in York. Betty and I each bought a Chinese Horoscope book,and I bought a Krishnamurti Reader. We bought tea and settled in the downstairs section of the cafe as the weather wasn't good enough to use the stylish sidewalk cafes. We saw Punk Rockers performing and a juggling act, both from a distance. After tea we went through a shop that sold old maps and prints. We rounded up the group at 2:45 at the Museum entrance and I sent Betty off with the bulk of the group, while

I waited for the last five. Four had gone to the toilet and left their friend to look after their bags.

We were all on the bus by 3pm sharp so we left returning past the National Theatre by the Waterloo Bridge. It seems a beautiful building. I'd have liked a closer look and a photo, oh well. We took a different route to the city's edge and arrived in camp about 5pm. After supper we adults were all invited to a wine and cheese party on the sub-camp -site where we had a chance to meet all the other adults involved in the sub-camp. There was a generous supply of food. We learned new songs and a dance that caught the sedentary type in the muscles, evidence of which was obvious for a couple of days. I didn't find it at all strenuous. It was Betty West's anniversary, so her son had sent her a bouquet of flowers, and she had a special cake. The sub-camp group worked together very well, and we were fortunate in this . Monday morning I went to help with the crafts on the sub-camp site for a couple of hours. I helped with nylon stocking doll faces while Connie did leatherwork and Judith flowers and butterflies. I began seriously working on my Chalk Hill Blues challenge. After lunch I babysat our site for a while. Doing this I found time to complete more of the challenges. Later I got ready for our trip to see 'Me and Myself' at the Adelphi Theatre. Supper was a superb, curry cooked by the East Indians. It was accompanied by Dahl and Rice. We had cake for dessert.

Sunday. After dinner I went down to the field after the balloon arrived. Betty was luckier than I as she managed to stand where they opened the fence for the queue, and was one of the first few to go up. I was close to the gate when they stopped for the night. As they chose the final few, my young friend, Ryan, hollered 'Jake why don't you take her?' It made me feel special, but embarrassed. Jake asked me to try again.

Saturday found us checking and filling water buckets, tidying the site and preparing for the Brownies to visit. They arrived around 10am. It was cold, so they were putting on an extra sweater, and long pants. We sang songs and I taught them AHKATAKANUVA, and shared in their sing-a-long. At some point Betty and I visited sub-camp HQ, and happened to meet the World Chief Scout, Garth Morrison accompanied by Bill James Sussex County Commissioner. Garth Morrison was a physically fit, young looking gentleman with wavy grey hair, and alert eyes, who wore his kilt with ease . It was a pleasure to speak with him.

After the Brownies left at 3pm Betty was still away having taken the Rangers for water sports, so I decided to wander around the campsite. I found the Canadians on the Bognor Regis site, the Germans next door, and then went to Mole in search of the Japanese. I met Hisako from Osaka, and traded addresses. Later I went to the Mole headquarters, and met their directors. There I noticed their mole toy kits, so went back for money, and returned to buy mine with Betty who also purchased one. We were given Mole patches and became acquainted with Rona Bingham who told us they were expecting a hot air balloon to come in,and rides would be 1st come 1st served. I also met a young lady whom I encouraged to apply as Cabana staff. Later we went to visit the Rangers, and Joy on Raven. They had had a much better lunch and supper than we had. Our lunch was bacon butties (sandwiches of bacon only, no lettuce or tomato) and a piece of fruit for dessert. Our supper for Saturday of Curry and cake, was not upstaged. They had had bacon quiche, a choice of fresh vegetables, and choice of desserts.

We went back to check out the barn dance in the Abergavenny building. It was terrible. Dust was flying, you could neither hear nor understand the caller and people either did their own thing or left. Joy and I left, Betty having vanished in the direction of the Rangers. Although it was cold, Joy, Pauline and I decided to teach the ten or so girls who were with us "I Let Her Go" and "T.I.R.O", and then we enjoyed hot chocolate and went to bed.

Sunday was lovely. The weather was cool. We slept a little later, had porridge, then scrambled eggs. We filled the water containers after washing up. Then went to the main arena area to learn some dance techniques from "Spring Break", a London-based Christian dance company. I couldn't do all of the routines, but enjoyed watching the ones I had too many left feet for. We went back to a lunch of salad bar, vegetables grated cheese, and bread with angel's light for desserts.

That afternoon we all turned up in full uniform for Guides'/Scouts' Own, a lovely simple service complete with universal songs, and three performances from the dance troop 'Spring Break'. Their performance of Zacchaeius (?) was carefully choreographed, and had an impact on the audience. It was exceptional. After the service some international groups performed, but there was no announcement that this would take place, so most of the crowd drifted off to collect their money to spend at the West Sussex Country Fair designed to raise money for Great Ormond St, a children's hospital in London that needs refitting. An amazing variety of stalls appeared on the field, some selling Welsh cakes, Scandinavian or Dutch pancakes with preserves. There were games of chance of every type, one fellow allowed you to autograph his jeans for 2p, others were dressed up as beggars and Peter Thomas who had been in charge of our sub-camp in 1980 was leading his cow and charging 2p to photograph your friend milking her. He was a delight in his farmer's smock. And he remembered me!

I was as in line to sample the wine and cheeses served by the ladies from Pitworth when he came by. The candy floss line must have been the longest. As I had been thirsty earlier, June Clark and I had stopped by the Rasp. Bread ladies from the Trefoil Guild who kindly offered us a cup of tea, and we made a contribution to Great Ormond St. From their area we had seen our East Indian group dance,as well as a French group dance and later the Norwegians. All in all it was a great day.

Tuesday Pauline and I went off with Freda in tow to check out the crafts offered in the Abergavenny building- brass rubbings, leatherwork, glass etching, pewter jewelry, patchwork, carved walking sticks and many others. We managed to settle in to learn how to make hedgehogs from teasel seed pods. They made beautiful Mrs Tiggleywinkles ornaments. We were all pleased with the results.

We had hot dogs for lunch (canned wieners) so I made up some muesli again. Betty and I had to be in uniform and ready by 12:30 for a 1pm trip to Arundel Castle. The trip went smoothly, we were dropped off at the carpark, the lady Venture Scout leader kept us together, paid the admission fees, and saw that we all understood where and when to meet for the return trip. The castle was a treasure of historical information. Not being a royalty buff, I hadn't realized that the Duke and Duchess of Norfolk were the highest ranking outside of the Royal Family, that they were Catholic, and had had this standing since 1066 following the Battle of Hastings. There were so many Thomas Howards that I lost track of them.

The furnishings were rare and of course the best money could buy. There were many exceptional paintings five or six Van Dykes, a Gainsborough, and many Dutch or Flemish Masters as well as works by several other outstanding English portrait artists The display explaining the family's involvement as High Admirals during various campaigns showed their abilities both as seamen and administration. They stated that it was Britain's careful planning that beat the Spanish Armada and Napoleon at Waterloo. The armouries was another interesting area. We saw many types of swords, lances and armour. We stopped to buy "stained glass" designs to colour, and I bought a guide to the castle to refresh my memory at a later date. We left the castle, stopping to take photos of the drawbridge and the moat. We hurried down the hill glancing at the antique store displays we passed. We went to the Art Exhibit near the car park where I bought a card. Then we worked our way back, and finally ended up in a shop called Cottage Antiques where I bought a set of six coffee spoons, and a small sauce ladle. We caught the bus which proceeded to take us almost to London before turning in the direction of the camp. Several people decided the driver didn't know where he was going,but he said he'd gone the long way to avoid rush hour traffic.

Supper that night was minced chicken and gravy with noodles and canned vegetables. As I believed they'd added onions and because I shouldn't eat noodles, I got two potatoes and two carrots that I grated up, mixed with an egg along with some of the chicken gravy then cooked like ham. It was quite tasty. As the others were having either apricot or cherry flan with banana or chocolate topping I had a serving of half a banana, half chocolate whip. After the dishes were washed, Betty and I were heading over to visit the Rangers when I heard them filling the hot air balloon. I raced over, and was I lucky I went up with the third group so I had my chance. I saw the camp from the air and a lot of the surrounding countryside. Someday I'm going on a balloon trip if I get the chance. Betty had arrived on time, and taken photos. We went back to visit the Rangers to use the hot water washrooms and to have a cup of coffee up in the Snack bar area.

It was a dry and hot Wednesday. In the morning we packed up our gear ready to take the tent down after lunch. We then cleaned up the dishes, and I went to the sub- camp marquee to burn a butterfly into a wooden spoon. There were two burners to choose from. I'd started out with one, but Jan came along and told me she preferred the other so I switched. I became so intent with my project that I didn't notice that the now unused burner was burning through the cord of the other. How embarrassing!! The one I was using had to be put away. Luckily it could be repaired. I was able to finish my spoon using the other burner.

I learned all I could about the chalk Hill Blue Butterfly so I was able to complete my challenge, and earn the spots on my butterfly, and my pennant. Our challenges had been reasonably difficult, but many on our site earned their pennants. After that we had to cheer for our groups on the sports field. They had 6 legged races, polo races, obstacle races, and a tug of war. We didn't win but we had a good time. I went back part way through to get some traders. At that time I decided to take- the sweatshirt I'd bought for Motoko to Hisako to take to Japan and the Ranger scarf (old style) to Rona Bingham who had got me in the balloon.

I met Helmie en route, and we discussed some of the shortfalls of the camp. Her girls had been disqualified twice due to the lack of a noticeable finish line- and it was sad knowing that they were leaving camp on a down note. I went back, and the sports day seemed a shambles. They really needed a megaphone to run it well. While I was running around, Betty had taken down the tent. Now we just had to load as much of Midhurst's things as possible into Betty's car after she had gone out to get the fish and chips for the Rangers. I offered to help but Glynnis had no jobs for me. However I was asked by Pauline to take Freda to trade with the other Canadians. I felt Freda should be able to do this herself- she reminded me of a whiny child. When Freda asked me herself I agreed- taking her to trade, taking a patch to Joy and going to wash my hair in the super washrooms (with hot water) in the pavilion building.

Finally Glynnis chose me to attend one of the two meetings for the closing ceremonies. I went to learn about the torches to be carried to lead the way to the fireworks display after the closing ceremony. I volunteered to help light the torches during the ceremony and pass them out and carry one.

Betty and I had been invited to supper by the Rangers so after I'd explained the closing ceremony procedure to all the guides I left for the Rangers' site. As I was doing a sheet of suggestions for the camp administrators I told the girls what I'd written and made a couple of critical generalizations for which I was quickly and carefully taken to task by "Henry"- she was right of course and I was glad to see some fighting British spirit. Nothing bothers me than people who always let you walk over them. Guess they remind me of a younger me.

And so ended my time at West Sussex '88. Soon I was home in Burnaby.

ADAM, YVETTE, LINDSAY, KELLY, KORI, AND RANDI

Chapter eight persons of interest
MarieRose, George's Aunt on his mother's side. Joan George's new wife
My daughters Nancy and Yvette George's sister, Ona

CHAPTER EIGHT

SORTING THINGS OUT

George had died March 28th. Nancy was in her second year of Architecture at UBC getting ready to write exams when he died. She still had books, clothes and personal effects in the house but Joan changed the locks so she couldn't get them.

Yvette was pregnant. Randi was about 13 months but for Yvette the incredible stress of losing her father and interchanges with her Aunt and Joan caused Yvette to miscarry losing the baby. Her Aunt Ona had taken the family keepsakes that Ona's mother and Grandmother had given us including the portrait photo of Ona's mother as a toddler that had hung over Yvette's bed most of her life. Her Aunt 's attitude was particularly nasty so I finally phoned her but she kept hanging up on me so I wrote her a letter telling her in no uncertain terms to keep out of our lives forever. I never saw her again until I went to George's Dad's funeral several years later. There were only about eight people there including family. Ona's husband did the eulogy. Pa was probably turning over in his grave. I was so disappointed that I went home and wrote this Eulogy to be read by Yvette at his service in Ste Rose Du Lac. He was a man of many talents.

Alfred Dheilly—Fred to his friends "Pa" to his family was an unusual man. He loved to argue, was opinionated and at times outspoken but he was a creative person with a tenacious, questioning mind. He grew up in a farming community where his carpentry skills were in demand. He was a formidable hunter who helped family and friends during the depression. He was an inventor who made something like a snowmobile years before anyone else ever thought of them. Whenever I needed a machine to solve a problem I'd ask him. He fixed cars, appliances and more. He was an entrepreneur remodeling houses or building them from the ground up. I learned from his son who learned from him. On top of this he travelled-back to France once or twice—to Mexico—across Canada, around the U.S. and he was still driving at 85---a lively opponent—a remarkable man.

Joan finally released Nancy's belonging. She could pick them up December 30th, they would be outside the front door. Nancy was leaving for Europe on the 31st. What pressure. Nancy decided to go alone to avoid any conflicts so she borrowed the KAL TIRE truck from Aunt Susie and went off to Squamish. There was too much to bring and to sort so she brought what she could and we sorted it later. This woman never even told the girls where or when she was putting George's ashes. They suggested the ashes be put near Marcia's ashes overlooking Howe Sound. Soon Nancy was off to Barcelona for a semester abroad.

Dear Zip,   *Dec.3/88*
Finally I'll get this long overdue letter on its way. It's so easy to put off writing, but time does go on, and oh so quickly. Hope you enjoyed your tour of Europe. Thanks for the card! I phoned Yvette a few nights ago wanted to make sure you were in Burnaby. She told me you were coming down Dec. 18th to Dec. 30th. Hope we get a chance to have a good chat. Hope you've got all the problems resolved.
Alfred was here this summer and I found him quite changed, his hands were very shaky, I was wondering if maybe he had Parkinson's.
Well, everyone is fine out here. It wasn't a good year though, hope we never have another like '88. Along with losing cattle; we had the drought and had to buy lots of hay and straw, and have new wells dug, ours cost me $3630.00 had to go 129 feet and still ended up with salt water, but then its for the cattle. And there was plenty of it so it is not so bad. Donald had to have another one dug, too

for the house, so he had the same deal, it's a bit salty, too but not as bad as ours.

Joanne+Donald's well ran dry too so he has to fill up the cistern which is not very big, so he's forever hauling water. Enough complaining now.

Donald and Gilles flew to Orlando on the first [Dec.] From there they'll be picked up to go on a cruise to the Bahamas at Port Canaveral. This was the trip Donald won while in Disney World last December. It was for two and wild horses couldn't drag Valerie out there. She says she gets sick on the plane, sick on boats and that was it! The boys will be back on the 9th. Hope they enjoy it. I was tempted to go with them but then we'd have to leave the place unattended for so long. Still have 20 chickens around, 3 cats and the dog .Denis is doing the rest of the chores.

The gardens turned out surprisingly well for such a dry year, the only thing that didn't turn out were the cucs, but Valerie had lots so I still got plenty.

Travis was one year old Nov. 30th and has been walking for about a month now. He's not very big, but sure gets around. Ashley is kept busy watching him.

My mother is in hospital where she'll be staying from now on, unless she gets into a nursing home. She's still quite good at 92, but Frank couldn't cope with all the care she needs now. She wants lots of company so I try to go at least every other day, We have choir practice once a week, and Renew meetings once a week, then I take Lisa, Aaron and Garrett for their Catechism lessons once a week [for 10 weeks] so it is all time consuming. There's no more religious teachings in school, so it has to be done by parents in the home.

Well, I'd better mosey along. Joanne phoned me and wants me to go over and have supper with them. She's got a bunch of fresh fish, so that sounds good, its kind of boring eating by myself here. Wishing you happy holidays and all the best in '89.

Love, Marie Rose

Chapter Nine persons of interest.
Glen, a young man severely injured in a car accident.

CHAPTER NINE

GLEN

I looked for work because I wasn't aware I could survive by being a substitute teacher. I accepted a job as a tutor/scribe for a student who had been in a car accident that left him brain damaged, physically challenged and struggling to have any kind of a life.

After they finished Grade Eleven a group of Glen's friends decided to go to Cypress Bowl. Glen caught a ride with one of his friends. They took some beer along. On the way out he went with his other friends. The driver didn't negotiate one of the curves so the car hit a tree. Glen was in the back seat wearing a lap seatbelt. He broke the back window with his head. He went forward cracking his ribs on the back of the seat in front of him. The driver, I believe, only had minor injuries. His girlfriend had a broken leg. Glen was in a coma for a couple of months. When he came to, he needed lots of physiotherapy. He needed help to retrain his hands, his legs and his brain—to create the best life possible for himself.

When I first met Glen he could only walk a few steps. He needed his wheelchair all the time. I picked him and his chair up every morning, and took him home after school. We attended North Delta High taking Law, Career and Personal Planning, and whatever else was necessary for him to graduate. Since he couldn't write he told me what his answers were and I wrote them down. We focused on courses where he could take part in the discussions. Glen had wanted to become an automobile mechanic.. He loved cars, had his own Chevy Camaro, and wanted to cruise around with the rest of his friends.

He had, also, been into body-building, lifting weights to increase his strength. Going back to lifting weights helped him to recuperate. He worked steadily on thinking positively, not blaming others, and getting physically stronger. He got to walk further, and further. He went from being irate, frustrated and immobile to being calmer, more patient with himself and others and able to walk with a cane even if he did still move like a wind up toy.

Fortunately he could still lift weights so he worked on getting his frustrations out through exercise. Glen's fantastic sense of humour really helped. We discussed many things, tried to keep on a positive track and became good friends. We travelled the halls of North Delta together. The day he decided to try walking upstairs was amazing, wonderful. Like most of us Glen varied from blaming the driver of the car he was in to blaming himself for deciding to ride with him and everything in between. Glen graduated from high school and went on to Kwantlen College to try to become a partsman in an automotive store.

During the summer holidays in 1989 I took Glen with me to visit Yvette and family in Manitoba. We explored the Portage la Prairie area, went out to Delta marsh, took in the corn festival in Austin where we checked out the old steam tractors and probably went off to Ste Rose du Lac, so I could catch up with Marie Rose and most of the Parthenays. When we came back to BC Glen checked in to Kwantlen. His knowledge of cars and mechanical problems was well above average, but his manual dexterity was poor due to brain damage. His voice was weak—-difficult to understand, so it soon became apparent he wouldn't be able to work in this field.

Glen's settlement came through. He was able to drive a modified vehicle, but he had to try several times before passing his road test. He kept lifting weights, going to the gym and was committed to training to compete in Summer and Winter Paralympic sports. He competed locally, provincially, nationally, and in many world-class weightlifting events. He helped out in gyms, and worked on keeping a positive attitude no matter what. He collected many medals, too. He bought himself a house and volunteered with the Paraplegic association helping fix wheelchairs.

SUSAN AND RAI ANN

Chapter ten persons of interest
My letter to Nancy is from Japan where I am visiting Motoko.
Susan another Crazy Woman   Lorena another young woman studying
at SFU

CHAPTER TEN

SUSAN

What a stroke of luck it was meeting Susan at the first Japanese conversation class I took in the Fall of 1983. Susan was young, vibrant, a go-getter well on her way to living life to the fullest. She studied and learned many Japanese customs before her and her current flame, a golf pro headed to Japan. I was leaving my husband, George and needed personal time and space to sort myself. Living with Motoko, a Japanese Girl Scout leader would meet my needs. I needed the classes' language and culture emphasis.

During the three and a half months I was in Japan Susan and I only exchanged a couple of phone calls. Both were positive, encouraging.

After I came back from Europe and West Sussex '88 we met again when we separately signed up for another Japanese class at UBC. We followed that with many international student functions and paired up when the BC Ministry of Education offered weekends of intensified Japanese or Chinese instruction. Susan's language skills were stronger than mine so we were in different classes. She worked for private schools that taught English to foreign students. Her cross-cultural awareness was a bonus for her employers.

I began working as a teacher on call [substitute], mostly in Delta. I applied for a full time position in Langley, but blew that chance when I told the interviewer he had too many rules. One and a half full pages! I had taken part of the Orton Gillingham method for teaching students with learning disabilities from the Fraser Institute, but too much time was spent on simple spelling procedures. It was too boring so I nodded off in class. I withdrew from that, too. The Academy had too many rules, too. I must wear a dress. I MUST chew boys out if their ties weren't straight and on and on. I didn't apply to work there, but I did go in as a teacher on call one day. I quickly learned the students names, created a cooperative mood, and taught the days lessons. At the end of the day I was offered future employment. No, thank you, not my style.

I was still tutoring students as the opportunities came my way. Around Christmas time Susan said there was an opening for an Art/ Social Studies/ ESL position at Dorset College. She advised me to apply, and recommended me to the Principal. Coming back to teaching must have brought out the best in me as I still have several students from my first class in January 1990 as friends. We get together whenever we can.

Dear Nancy,   *3-9-41 Someji*
                      Chofu-shi 182, Japan   *.26/6/89*

      Lost a day crossing the date line-sure gets you older faster and cuts down on your free time. Your life sounds like it is progressing well. Think your gift for Kori will be just right. Yvette says his hair is strawberry blond so he may have a little of his Aunt in him.

I'm glad your flat is no smoking. My house is except for Ray. Katsu and Minoru are both great to have around. The more I get to know Katsu the better I like him.

The more I get to know Minoru the more puzzled I am. I hope he gets his act together while I'm away. Just discovered that he has two ulcers the other day and I've been teasing him, of course. Hope he finds a job he likes. Katsu has bought a 1977 Celica in excellent shape all things considered. He's lined up a job as a dishwasher. They are both going to the Harper's 50th Wedding anniversary tea today and they will come to the family picnic the day I come home so I told them to have a picnic lunch packed and to pick me up at the airport. Wouldn't want to waste any time. Ray asked me to find the COMPLETE BOOK OF ZEN for him so I'll take a stab at it.

His life is still 2 steps forward 1 step back but I love him as he is. Your professional exchanges with Yasmin must be interesting.

Minoru loves curry and Somnuk had us out for an excellent Thai meal. She never has figured out that I can't eat garlic or onions so I had to miss a lot of the meal and her friend who cooked it felt bad [so did I....I need to look after me. Lorena had the yellow car towed to Canadian Tire and I had them adjust the timing, replace the distributor cap, replace the new spark plugs as they said they were the wrong type and put in a new voltage regulator which was running the battery down. Now it should have a new battery they tell me –but I said $100 is enough for now especially as I don't know if Minoru will drive it or not. So it is still registered in Lorena's name and I gave her $60 to put standing insurance on it. If Minoru decides to use it he can arrange it with Lorena. I know he understands as I got him to explain it back to me. I haven't done anything about your other car yet. Joanne Fern came and got her car. She's working downtown.

I haven't seen her as she kept leaving messages on my machine but no phone number so I still have her boxes, her car key and her huge portfolio—if she needs them I told her to try to catch Katsu or Minoru. Lorena bought an '81 Mustang in wine/rust tones—I think it suits her. She said we should take Katsu and Minoru to the PNE when I get back. Grace will be down then, Liz has a job at a muffin shop. Think Susie has decided no more $40 a week down the drain on piano lessons and I think she's right. Now it is up to Liz. Alex is in the Summer Games again and then they are all off to Hawaii after that. Alex is the neatest guy.

Got the back blacktopped so it is all neat and clean. Either Ray or the guys will keep the place up. Paul, Ray. Minoru and I went for supper Friday and Ray, Katsu, Minoru and I went to the Irish Rovers 25th Anniversary due and kicked our heels. They told me they couldn't dance but I know differently now. I asked Yvette to send you a copy of the house plans. I'll need a roof line, foundation [plus crawl space usage?—Paul said I should extend the basement—I don't think so—now any advice, suggestions, etc., etc. I told him I'd ask God!].

This storage space could hold a root cellar for potatoes, etc-a wine cellar for the next owners—garden equipment, or, or.

The only thing I'll need is an extra tap to water the garden. Do you have any suggestions as to windows, etc. Yvette put in a lot of glass block above the countertops and at the top of walls for light transference. I told her it is probably too expensive and Paul says I don't gain too much light in the bathrooms. Do you know which are the bearing walls?

Yes, I'm now officially ROXSANE TIERNAN—didn't have time to change my passport, etc. so left all that till after Japan. Have Shaun's sisters in the house in Langley and cheques for next year. I can't see further down the road than that. Motoko and two of her friends had a welcome sushi dinner for me last night. My first student and another came today bringing a delicious lunch with them. Tomorrow I'm going to learn something about Japanese writing. The next day I'm going to learn a new craft. We plan to walk to a special display of Japanese iris, to go for a couple of picnics to take a night cruise of Tokyo Harbour, To visit Nikko, a few Guiding events and 4 days with my friends in Machida. I've read most of a book on Japanese festivals today as well as finishing off the book "ACROSS CHINA by Peter Jenkins That I read on the plane. I need to start writing my books soon. I need to get myself in the right mood. My friends said I seem much healthier than I did in 1984.

They think Roxsane may be good for me.

Thursday I'm one kimono richer. I came heavy with books for friends and thought I'd go home lighter. Dreaming I was.

Hope all is well. Expect at least one super long letter when I get home. Have a great summer. Loads of Love, Mom

Think I've got the English section of the first book ¾ done. Now to keep plodding along.

PS Motoko sends her love, at Motoko's till the 13th then c/o the YMCA Hotel, Sannomiya, Kobe, Japan.

MRS. NOSE, EMI KITAZONO, CHIE DOMOTO in Kobe

Dear Nancy,   *July 26, '089*

I just came back from dinner at Sushi Boy—the Japanese automated, inexpensive sushi restaurant.

This host family is great. Emi speaks English very well. Her husband, Fukuyoshi, is a great help-he's gone to no end of patience explaining the cassette-recorder—in Japanese of course. AIWA that I bought for about $138. I'll be able to operate it like a pro someday. Koji is 12 [boy] and Maki [girl] is 15. She's too shy and embarrassed but kind—Koji has your kind of book cover-seems aggressive but really quite considerate.

Susan and I live about 2 minutes apart. We bike 20 minutes to the station everyday and back, of course. Then we take a 40 minute subway ride, 10 min.walk and we are at the YMCA. Between the riding and the two or three times a week I go with Susan and lift weights I'll be in better shape when I get home. Went to Toji market last Friday and bought Kori a lovely silk boys kimono. Couldn't find a really special one for Randi but got quite a cute polyester padded one anyway.

Our schedule is heavy and I've decided not to do some things I've done before.

Susan, Kathy and I went to a party at the Canadian Consul General's here in Kobe—a very enjoyable evening even if we broke curfew and had the guy at the desk in a flap. We'd have been later except the subway shut down at midnight.

I've taken about eight rolls of slides and have about 4 more to go. Should be able to make a great book or two. I'm going to have a lot of interesting experiences in this life. I'll have flower arranging lessons this week, a tea ceremony next week, a party this Saturday after the Kitano International Festival and we will probably go to a karaoke bar next week and who knows what else. Of course I'm studying hard. I do want to learn more. I have to give a three minute speech in Japanese next Monday. Maybe I'll do a dry run on what I'll tell the Girl Scout leaders in Osaka on Wednesday afternoon. I'm going around Kobe with a couple of 20-22 year old Girl Scouts next Saturday. Life is full of challenges and opportunities—even Roxsane has a style and reputation to live up to now.

I'm really curious as to what's going on in your world. Hope you've written me a really long letter and mailed it ! I put the lock on the bike here. You know I can do some mechanical things. Hope I can get a good job when I go home. If not I'll just keep my houses fully rented and enjoy life with part time work.

Yesterday at the homestay's we had sushi, deep fried prawns and salad followed by a delicious dessert, beer, wine and hot water for me. The daughter played the mandolin beautifully so we had a great sing a long. The father's car is even more automated than Allen's. That family has every new gadget including a laser disc TV and a fantastic sound system.

Went to the Matsushita Museum of Technology- you never know what will be invented next. I took a picture of their kitchen.

Hope all is well. I may take a two week course in methods when I get back. It starts the day after I arrive. Must think about that.
Loads of Love, Mom

Dear Crazy Woman,
Sorry I've been so busy. THANK YOU, THANK YOU, THANK
YOU. San Diego was wonderful—what an opportunity. I really
enjoyed the experience- meeting Georgina and Wanda, the other
staff, students and seeing you again.

My grand children loved Disneyland. Kori said it was the best
day of his life [all 6 years of it]. Hope my pictures turn out. Should
get some back today.

Now—I, also, feel remiss in not encouraging you to buy the
rug from Oaxaca when we were in Tijuana. Buy one in any colour
combination that you love. You will always find a place for it.
They do wear well. The Talavera pottery is beautiful BUT may
break like any other pottery/china so unless you can cushion it
well the rug is the better buy at $100 to $125 US. The small rug
I have on my dining room wall is 20 inches by 30 inches and we
paid $26 for it in Oaxaca in 1986.

I'm back at work. Hoping all will go well. Loads of Love,
Roxsane and Bill

Nancy added at the top of her letter. Thanks for the cheque,
now I have to figure out what to get, think perfume on the way
home sounds fine. Thanks again.

Hi Mom,   *Sept 24, 89*
Well, now I am becoming older & wiser[?] Oh, of course, I'm
wiser anyway still no grey hairs even if Brian is trying to give
them to me.
Well, I didn't go to Milan, it would have been great but Wen,
Brian's flatmate was being a bag and her new beau Clinton wasn't
coming and I didn't feel like putting up with her on my holiday
so didn't go. Actually think it was wise we would have all been
miserable or I would have gone off and done my own thing and
Brian and Wen would have felt guilty. Anyway, didn't go. Will go
somewhere else instead, I think alone.
What did I say to baffle Raf yet once more? I'm sure something
he thought sounded strange. Anyway how is he doing? I guess as

you spoke he is still working in Van. Where is Joanne, I need her address, Do you have it

Cath called me two weeks ago to talk about Barcelona. She put both of our names down now must wait to hear back from them to see what they decided as 40 odd people applied and only 22 can go. Hopefully I get on that list and Cath, too. Must wait and see. She said she'd call as soon as it happened.

Definitely I think my love life is on hold till next summer or so. Brian is still trying but being in Milton Keynes is good for me, a bit of distance.

Here on your birthday you bring cakes for everyone in the office. So I am going to bake chocolate chip cookies, should be novel for them.

I usually go down to London every weekend but next weekend will stay in MK Me and some people from the office can go out and party. On the 7ᵗʰ Yaz and the London bunch are taking me out for dinner which will be fun.

I went out with most of the London office on Friday for a Russian meal which was good. One of the director architects is leaving soon to set up on his own so was nice to have a chat although I'm sure I will see him again. Spent Saturday with Denise the new secretary in London, nice kid, she is 21 and very full of life. Everyone here thinks I'm 19-21 or so. I'm regressing and that's even with my face on.

Yaz has a cold so wasn't out-will see her on the 7ᵗʰ I guess.

Elizabeth did write me but she never mentioned getting anything at all so as long as they got it that's fine.

Haven't really contemplated your plans much putting in a basement will be expensive and we really don't need more storage. The glass block sounds nice but could be expensive. Check around at scrap yards Maybe you should see how much it costs, how much you can find and then decide where to put it, I'm sure you'll enjoy the tub.

London to Vancouver Wardair flight 127 28 Nov. 2:45 pm

Well a bit later, did go to London. Brian took me to see the Magic Flute at the ENO which was great. He got good seats so I would dress up and wear my black dress. Then he took me to a lovely little French restaurant all in all a wonderful evening. Then Sunday went out with Steve from MK office to see a Bolivian Indian band which was very good. Then Monday went out with Brian [from the office] and Jim for dinner and a good chat. I didn't make chocolate chip cookies I bought them. They gave me flowers and a few desk toys to fiddle with when on the phone.

I got on the list for Barcelona. Supposedly we have to be in Barcelona ready For class on Jan. 3rd. Will fly back to London and then either fly or train it to Barcelona. I can leave my bike here and some stuff so I can travel lighter. Next summer Brian wants me in London and Jim wants me back here and Jojo sounds a bit disappointed with her love life but the job sounds good and rewarding. Think the two of us should stop looking and trying so hard and just wait for something to happen in the love life area. Got a letter from Yvette and she never mentioned getting anything either but I know from you she did. Some peoples kids.

Anyway, I should go hope all is well. If I find the plans [think they are at Brian's will look this weekend] will send more info. Lots of Love Nancy say hi to every one.

Hi Zip,   *Dec 12/89*

Well, I'm sure you're not finding the time long these days, with your two girls home and two grandchildren. I'm sure the two weeks will just fly. Kori is a cute little fellow and Randi is a real doll.

Well, I'm still not all set for Christmas. I spent 3 days in Winnipeg last week and next week we'd like to go to Minot for 3 days if Cecile is feeling better and if the weather can warm up a little. Tonight it is -35 and we finally got a little bit of snow to hide the black snow we had after a dust storm 2 weeks ago. How's Nancy? Glad to be home I'll bet and I'm sure the two of you are spoiling the little ones. That's what grandmas are for. I'm babysitting Ashley and Travis. Joanne and Donald have gone to Laurier, the basement is made for their house and they are putting more flax straw so the cement won't freeze. They're hoping to frame it this winter and take it from there next summer.

Well, hope this finds you all well as we are. Have a terrific Christmas and all the best in 90.

Love from all, Marie Rose

FromK.

P.S. I have a strange news to tell you! One day in January this year, a letter happened to be sent to the wine shop near my house [down below the slope]—perhaps you can remember. The letter was written by two primary school children named C and L.. They said that they found a pigeon in Naniamo, Canada. The pigeon had a ring around the leg so they could find its owner. [Mr F. who is the owner of the wine shop] by its number. It is sure that the number of the ring that the pigeon had is one of Mr. F's pigeons. It has been missing for about one year, since it took part in the 222km. race in Japan. Maybe the pigeon lost its way at that time. But why? Why was it found in Canada very far from Japan? Too far for it to fly! It must be impossible! Mr. F said that it flew over the sea and took a rest on one of the sailing vessels and was kindly helped.

Mr F said that it got the first prize in 143 km. race. It is one of the best pigeons he keeps, but he doesn't want it to be sent back again to him because it is not good for the pigeon. He hopes they will keep it and love it.

So I wrote the letter to the children, told them what Mr.F wanted. It was more than two months ago But they haven't answered him yet. So he is worrying. Can you check with the school and the two students and get them to tell you and me about the pigeon.

I'm glad to tell you my friends are all fine as is my family,

We did learn the students had looked after the pigeon.

Motoko

Chapter Eleven persons of interest
Emi, my host mother in Kobe Chie Domoto, a friend of Emi and I
Mal, another teacher at Dorset College Gary, Susan's boyfriend
Kuniko Iyama, a mentor of mine who did all the illustrations for
CELEBRATE JAPAN.
Bill the love of my life.

Danny Tsang at top; Andy Lam at bottom students at Dorset

CHAPTER ELEVEN

TEACHING AT DORSET

I'll never forget that first class-Danny, Dickson, Xenon, Anne, Rebecca, Andy and another Rebecca and Edith plus seven more. I remember explaining to the class how ticked off I was when Andy told me he had an appointment with the Principal, but he was really cutting class to go help a friend find her lost dog! I need my students to be honest with me. I cannot help them if they are not. The message got to Andy and Rebecca quickly. He came back and apologized. They found Rebecca's dog. That class went for Dim Sum together several times. I remember them following me along the Sea-to-Sky Highway; walking through the bush above Smoke Bluffs to see the view of Squamish. Later we went to Alice Lake for hot dogs cooked over an open fire—-they were afraid to eat them. They didn't think the grill was clean enough, and had never cooked over an open fire. But they were impressed that I could walk through the bush, and I could use an axe as well. I had picked up the axe to split the wood and kindling. They thought I was Superwoman. Camping in BC was nothing like living in Hong Kong or Taipei.

In 1990, Susan and I were awarded bursaries by the BC Ministry of Education to study Japanese at the YMCA in Kobe, Japan, off we went. Coincidentally our homestay families were out in the boondocks, but we were only a few houses apart. We borrowed bicycles from our host families and rode back and forth from the train station in the humid, sweaty heat of summer in Japan. I made a great friend of my homestay Mother who is at least twenty years younger than me. Emi, my homestay mom, took me to see "Kuwaite Sorro". She was so star struck by the lead actor that she nearly fell over the rail of our loge seats. She, also took me out to dinner and for an evening of dancing in the company of a woman known as "the Queen of Sannomiya". I have been back to see her a couple of times.

HOT DOGS AT ALICE LAKE

One of the requirements of the bursary was to prepare lesson plans. Instead I wrote a book CELEBRATE JAPAN self published that Fall when I was back teaching at Dorset.

The book was illustrated by my friend Kuniko Iyama who was happy when I asked her if I could use her art work and still happy when I told her I needed four more illustrations. The information about the annual festivals and traditions in Japan mostly came from times I spent with Kuniko in Japan in 1984 so maybe she or I was a ghost writer. The books are a timeless resource for Grade Five or Six Social Studies.

Dear Roxsane,   *May 1, 1990*

    I have just received our books! What an exciting day today is! I don't know how many thanks I should say to you. I'm very happy and thankful to have the fasicnating books, and I'm glad to be a little useful for you with my illustrations. Masahiko and Mitsue are surprised and also pleased. Mitsue is sending you her baby's photo with a short message. Of course, Yukio is very grateful. I'll write to you before long. Kuniko

Dear Roxsane   *July 19th.*

    Thank you very much for your writing book. I received it on the 16th of July. It's very fast by airmail. I was very surprised your special book. How wonderful! Mrs.Kuniko's drawing pictures are very good. Those had warm heart, and your explanation was easy to understand. It will be very interesting to many foreigners. Of course, Japanese, too. I showed it to my friends. They were deeply impressed to the contents of the book and they want to order the book so fast. Please send me 21 books. As fast as you can by air mail. Today I send you $24 Canadian for my book.
After 21 books arrived to my house I will send you all books money at once. I'm looking forward to receiving the books.
Good-bye love Chie

At Dorset I specialized in Canadian Studies, History, Geography, Economics and Law as well as Fine Arts. My first classes of students mainly from Taiwan and Hong Kong became long term friends. I've been to their graduations, weddings and when they are in town they bring their children to visit. Those first classes became a large family for me really enriching my life. One morning I remember them leaning over the mezzanine railing chanting "rock, rock, Roxsane". It was embarrassing but it sure made me feel good. We got together for Dim Sum, each paying for our own meals. On Mother's Day they bought me a china turtle, a symbol of long life.

    Another Dorset College class went skating at Riley Park. I had rarely skated before but one of the smallest students from Hong Kong came along, took my hand saying "Come on Missy". Soon I was skating freely.

At Dorset I became the sponsor for the Student's Council. They put on dances at the Ukrainian Catholic Church hall that was nearby. Keeping up with the current dances and the energy of the students kept me in shape. The next day was a very emotional one for me.

It started off with the first group of students and staff going skiing: 90 off to Mount Seymour. Then getting ready for the 82 students and staff that would go the next day and supervising a catch all class of English 2 students who didn't go skiing. Later they watched the video RIEL in Social Studies 10 and discussed 'biases'. After school I solved problems with the list for Seymour Mountain, a whale watching problem, returned the video to the Film Board downtown and delivered books to the Pac Rim Slide Show people..

Later I gobbled down some Sushi for dinner; had a chocolate bar for dessert and checked on Masa my home stay student from Japan. He was working in a Japanese souvenir store in the mall at the Hyatt Regency complex. I was admiring something in a store window when L K, Marcia's former boyfriend appeared out of nowhere. A ghost to catch up with. L had dated Marcia, my youngest daughter, before she died of a brain tumour. He was now a Forestry Engineer working for International Forest Products. At a recent safety meeting the Workmen's Compensation Safety presenter went over George's death—this was especially rough for him—I haven't seen him since. My emotions were really high. I had a hard time getting to sleep that night.

I taught at Dorset until a student driving his girl friend to Whistler lost control of his car. His girl friend died. Her death saw our college's registrations in Hong Kong drop by just over two hundred students.

DANNY GRADUATES FROM SFU.

When I left on holiday June '91 I was tenth from the bottom of the seniority list. When I came back I had no job. Luckily for me the Dorset Administration was able to pass on information from Mal a teacher who had moved on, that there was a position open in the New Westminster International Studies section. I went home picked up my resume, delivered it by 2pm and passed the 8pm interview. I was employed again teaching ESL, English as a Second Language.

Susan met Gary about this time. I met Bill in August 1992. Susan and Gary were both qualified teachers. They reassessed their lives and decided to take their Master's Degrees at San Diego State University. Having completed their degrees in 1995 Susan became the coordinator for SDSU's Summer Session for 250 Italian students seeking a program in ESL. When she was filling her staff positions she invited me to come and teach for three weeks. Susan arranged our [Bill's and my] sub-lease of the apartment usually rented by one of her students who had gone home for the summer. All went well until we got to the border and were turned back. I contacted Susan who managed to smooth things out.

Bill and I drove to my cousin's in Lake Forest California. Sarah, my cousin took me to get the social insurance work permit approved. I went to work.

The students really enjoyed creating fabulous tales of where, why and with whom the absentee students were away. It was a good way to keep the students using their English. Of course, we tackled their grammar and phrasing, too.

One weekend the four of us went to Tijuana. Bill and I wore our brightest clothes so Susan and her friend Georgina could not lose us. We all had a great time. I had a chance to show off my Spanish, too. Next we checked out the beaches near SDSU a few times. Watching Susan and Gary we knew that they had found the their mates for life.

A couple of years later after Susan had miscarried five or six times they decided to adopt a baby girl from China. I had no hesitation in recommending these two as parents. They are both teachers trained as Physical Education/Counseling majors. They are both very active, very kind, responsible citizens who really care. Rai Ann graduates in 2018 and her sister Alana, Susan and Gary's natural daughter, will graduate next year, I think. What a family.

Chapter Twelve persons of interest
Shirley my house-renovating partner and good friend
Don a handyman/carpenter friend My youngest sister Grace

1988 BECOMING AN ENTREPRENEUR 1988

Before I left Lucas Centre I applied for and got a mortgage on a house in Langley that had been rented to someone with kids who wrote on the walls with crayons, peed on the carpets, and generally left the house a disaster. Shirley and I worked as a team on this our first venture into the real estate market. I always admired Shirley as she could handle the twists and turns of life. She had studied at Blanche McDonald's school of beauty. Sometimes I envied her confidence and her sense of style. I knew she could make her own cheese, buy antiques as an investment and tackle home repairs including plumbing and electrical. After all, I had watched as she bought a place in Squamish at the tax sale. She poured her heart and soul into getting that place exactly how she wanted.

JOHN AND I ON THE ROOF—addition to my house.

I could clean, paint and redesign adding practical touches, and I looked after the contracts, and purchasing. Shirley handled anything to do with electricity, and plumbing. It took us six weeks of weekends to get the house marketable. We painted, put in new carpets, and a new kitchen countertop. I tried to sell it myself but it wasn't to be. After six weeks trying to sell it we decided to lease it to friends of a friend. Shirley and I sat back, and waited. I'd had an open house for the local realtors who told me we had done a great job, and that the price was right. Shirley and I kept busy. I collected the rent, and paid the mortgage. By this time, I was busy working full time as a tutor for Glen. I was shocked when a realtor phoned, "Is your place still for sale? I think I have a buyer."

My response, "Sorry I've leased it for a year."

"Mmm, I think I can work with that." So, he got permission from the tenants to show the house. It didn't appeal to the first prospect but the second one thought it was great. The realtor helped the tenants get resettled and sold the house for twenty five thousand more than I had asked for it. There was a real estate boom just starting.

Soon I was looking for another place to remodel but I knew it had to be farther out from town. The prices continued to rise.

Selling the house in Langley gave me the funds to start over in Mission as Langley was now out of my price range. I bought a two bedroom full basement home with a carport. We turned the carport into a master suite with a large bedroom and full bath. Shirley hired a contractor to do the construction, and a plumber/electrician to do the rest. Shirley and I worked on dry walling the basement, cleaning, and painting. Part way through I had a funny feeling that something wasn't being done properly so one weekend I took Shigenori, one of my homestay students, and Anne Chen with me to help paint. Before we headed back to Burnaby, I got Shige and Anne to secure the ladder while I climbed up with a flashlight, and camera. That contractor had not put ANY insulation in the ceiling or walls. I was shocked. Of course, I phoned, fired him, and hired a Maple Ridge firm to blow insulation in. Shirley and I completed the work, but again it didn't sell easily so I rented it for a few years, and sold when the market picked up again.

During the renovations, as I was teaching full time, I usually threw a sleeping bag, enough food for the weekend, any tools, paint or whatever else we might need in the car Thursday night or Friday morning and headed out right after school on Friday. I would work till nine or ten at night with Shirley. We would start at it early Saturday morning, and keep at it till our energy ran out. Sunday we worked till about 2 pm. We kept this schedule over and over until the renovations were done. It usually took about 6 weekends. Shirley knew more about plumbing and electrical work than I did, and she could let trades people in during the week when necessary. It was a great partnership.

THE REST OF THE HOUSE WAS WORSE!

You really can't imagine anyone living in the next house I bought [with Yvette's money] in Mission. It was Spring, and Shirley was restless, so she suggested looking around Mission for another house to fix up. I didn't think we could afford another place as we hadn't sold the one on 7th yet. Yes, it was rented but we didn't have enough cash to put up a twenty or twenty-five percent down payment to secure a mortgage. We drove around checking things out anyways. The only place that interested me was an old house that had been barged up the river, and put on a foundation that was on two adjoining lots. The property included three lots facing Horne street. I checked out the price, got the realtor to show me inside, and then phoned Yvette to see what she thought. She had just inherited some money from her Dad's estate.

I told her the place was a disaster. The roof had been leaking for years. The cobwebs hung down four feet from the ceiling, and there was garbage everywhere. But, there were three lots so we should be able to get our money back come hell or high water.

If she put up the money I couldn't include Shirley even though there would be tons, and I mean TONS of work.

She agreed, so I put in an offer with the condition that the owner would see that the tenant's goods would be removed. He agreed, so we went ahead. I secured the mortgage with Yvette's money. I had a huge industrial garbage bin delivered to the back door. I hired some of Nancy's friends to clean out the house that had eighteen inches of garbage in most rooms. Then I got them to tear off the existing roof. We tore out the carpets, and some of the kitchen cupboards. I took pictures of every room before we started. Then we chopped down the evergreens that blocked the front windows. When we had everything under control, I had the bin picked up. I paid the bill and took it to the office of the previous owner. His secretary said, "He'll never pay that." So I dug out the photos. She took them in, and came back with the cheque.

Yvette and I decided to put a dormer on the house, an upstairs bathroom, a new roof, a new kitchen countertop, new paint and a small sundeck on the back. I thought we could probably sell the extra lot if necessary. I was back to my routine of leaving school Friday to work all weekend to make the place liveable.

I hired Don who had worked on my place in '89 and used the same plumber and electrician we had used on 7th. Yvette drove out with the kids and helped out. When we stopped at my sister Grace's for dinner she said, "Don't ever let Roxsane use your money. She buys garbage." Yvette laughed.

It took a while and a lot of labor. I went to the Carpet Warehouse in Clearbrook and bought wall to wall carpet for the bedrooms and living room. Soon it was rentable.

The tenants presented as a couple with four kids, and reliable references. When Fall came the basement leaked slowly in a few spots. I did some research, bought some Xipex and sealed the popcorn concrete. A month or two later, I realized the couple had split up and sometimes the rent was late.

In early February I got a call from a fellow who wanted to know if I owned the property at Second and Horne and if I was willing to sell it. I told him he wouldn't like my price, so he suggested meeting at White Spot on Lougheed at 7pm on Tuesday. We met. It turned out he wanted to build an office/facility that he could rent to the government on a permanent basis. I explained that the tenant had a one year lease and that I wanted $300,000 plus salvage rights. He agreed that my price was too high, but he said he thought he could work it in to the tender. He did, and he handled relocating the tenant, too.

About that time the tenant on 7th was having problems keeping his upholstery business going. In the end he recovered my chesterfield and chair with fabric I had bought in order to pay his last months rent, and they moved on. I think of that fellow whenever I consider reupholstering the sofa and chair. I love the colour and pattern of the fabric, and it has served me well even though he told me he didn't think it would last three years. That was 1991. It is now 2018 and yes, it shows some signs of wear..

When those folks moved on I put the house on 7th Street on the market. It sold so I squared up with Shirley. Almost every time I drove out to Mission I would take Anne or Johnson with me. It is a long way and I crave company.

We paid off the mortgage and bought two Mission houses that were in very good shape. We barely broke even on them. That's life.

JOANNE BECOMES ROXSANE.

Chapter Thirteen persons of interest
Fran, my friend from Chapter one

CHAPTER THIRTEEN

CHANGING TIMES;
CHANGING MY NAME

Sometimes tiny chance changes turn one's life in a different direction. One day in 1989 Fran and I were driving up Oak Street past the Kabalarian Centre. The sign read DISCOVER THE IMPACT YOUR NAME HAS ON YOUR LIFE Tuesday at 7pm here. We agreed it would be fun, so we decided to attend. As we went in the door, we had to fill out strips of paper with our full name and maybe our birth date. One would be drawn and presented that night. I kept telling myself it had to be mine. They started with my first name Edith. It indicated that I would see a lot of suffering but not be able to help. My middle name [the one I used], Joanne, meant I would work hard and get little credit.

My last name was what clinched my decision to change my name— all of it. The last name Dheilly meant everyone would be jealous. I thought about my husbands family. Jealousy was everywhere. If you borrowed tools from one the other was upset because you didn't borrow from them. I started the process. I found a first name easily. Then I got a list of thirty or so surnames that could work. I chose one that sounded Irish. With coaching I added an initial rather than a second name. This was to allow me to collect things, money, friends.....When I had it all in order I applied to the Department of Vital Statistics to change my name. I paid the fees, put notices in the papers, got my name registered, then contacted the banks, the University, all the necessary agencies and my friends. Hydro was the stickiest of all, and the friend that was with me at the beginning was one of the few who fought the change. My mother said okay, as did the majority of my friends, young and old. Some thought I had really flipped, lost my mind. Whether it was because I willed it, or because the economic times had changed or because people's perceptions had changed; no one has a definitive answer, but my life steadily improved. I know that for most things, I could be determined that the change would be positive. However, I cannot explain how after being afraid of heights- even painting in a stairwell was a challenge— now I was able to go up on roof, and comfortably lay out the shingles for Don to nail in place. I have no answer for that.

I changed my name in 1989 before starting back teaching, before publishing CELEBRATE JAPAN and three years before meeting Bill, the love of my life.

I sent off the following letter: *"The time has come the walrus said to talk of many things—Of why the sea is boiling hot— and whether pigs have wings..." I always liked Lewis Carroll's writing and the above passage came to mind when George and I were wandering over miles of black, solidified lava in Hawaii. It seemed to me that there was one place that the sea would have been boiling hot and pigs would have needed wings. Well what I am about to do may seem as strange to many of you as the above passage. I am going to change my name. From now on I will be Roxsane Tiernan. I am beginning a new section of my life—I will put the past behind me and not worry about the future (to the best of my ability). I hope you will all celebrate this new beginning with me.*

I have been very busy this spring. A friend and I have remodelled a house. The only thing we contracted out was having new carpets and flooring installed. The sale is to be completed on April 20th. Since we finished the house in Langley I have had the overgrown shrubs around my house removed and begun to re-landscape my lot. I have my lawn mower in to have its motor rebuilt. The grass will be too high when it comes back but maybe the rain will be gone. I have installed blinds in the dining room and yesterday I had an electrician check out the electrical system and install two light fixtures.

I have just finished a course on English as a Second Language and will begin one more at the beginning of May with luck. I took a Tai Chi course and managed to get to see most of the good movies that are showing this Spring- "Another Woman", "Beaches", "Cousins", Mississippi's Burning", and "Rainman". I also, went to another Intensive weekend in Japanese so my Japanese doesn't disappear like the dinosaurs.

I made Yvette a large collage of Tulips in Japanese Washii paper for her birthday. She is doing well. Her baby is due May 21. Randi was two on March 31,1989. She talked to me on the phone for the first time. Before she just listened. Yvette made her a castle out of refrigerator boxes. It has heart shaped windows and ivy crawling up it. I wish I could see it but I guess pictures will have to do. Nancy is fine. She worked for 3 weeks as a temporary in an Architectural office in London and then went to visit a friend in Holland and met her friend's cousin in Amsterdam. I hope she sends a letter soon...

Chapter Fourteen Persons of interest
My middle sister Susie, Yvette and Nancy
Homestay students Katsu and Minoru from Japan
Bill, Fran's son–in- law [I hadn't met my Bill yet.]

CHAPTER FOURTEEN

CHANGING TIMES 1990

When I turned fifty Susie and her girls had a birthday party for me. I was overjoyed. My girls were unable to come. Nancy was working in England, and Yvette and Allen lived in Portage la Prairie raising Randi and Kori. They had a delicious supper. Susie's girls chose the music according to their taste, and a good time was had by all even Rugrat, their tiny dog.

Yvette had been busy ahead of time. Randi helped her make fancy lollypops that looked like stained glass, but unfortunately they didn't survive being sent by mail. However, the chocolate covered popcorn cake with Smarties, and peanuts inside was impressive and delicious. Imagine getting a birthday cake in the mail!. We had a wonderful time, one that I will never forget.

Before Christmas that year Yvette with three year old Randi and one year old Kori came out for a pre Christmas visit.. As they arrived the same day as Nancy we all killed three hours at the airport waiting for Nancy's arrival. Keeping the little ones happily occupied was a challenge but driving home to turn around come right back made no sense. When Nancy finally arrived she barely said "hello" before leaving with her friends. Yvette, the kids and I went home disappointed. Before Yvette and her children went back to Portage, Nancy informed me that she was spending Christmas with one of her close friends. I was stunned, but a close friend, Shirley had been having problems with an adopted First Nations teen who went back to be with her birth mother on skid road. These friends were distraught . They had raised the girl and her brother since they were six and four. Now, at fifteen, she had been convinced by her 'friends' to get back to her 'culture'. So, I asked if Katsu, Minoru and I could go to Christmas dinner at their place.

That was good for all of us. What the girl really wanted to know was that her birth mother loved her. Unfortunately this led to an adult life using drugs and in prostitution. Terrible.

After Christmas Nancy went back to Europe. I waited until she sent a letter in June saying what a great time she had at Christmas to tell her how I felt about Christmas without her. I was very honest.

That year I was beginning to have more confidence in myself. After Christmas I went shopping for a new car. I asked Lisa's Bill to go with me as I felt he knew more about cars than I did. I had done my research at the library checking out "Lemon Aid" and other "Consumer Reports". We settled on a Toyota Tercel, a hatchback, a very practical car. I didn't buy the one at Budget which had only 17,000 kilometers on it as it looked like it had been through the mill. Instead I opted for the one at Hertz with 32,000 kilometers as it looked well cared for and had better quality tires. It turned out to be a wise choice.

At this time in my life I was trying to understand myself better. I attended several self help exploratory weekends. Weekends that taught one to believe in a positive life; one where if you wanted a Lincoln car you just had to believe that you would find a way to get one. I remember Don telling me you attract what you think about—for example if you worry about being robbed you might be robbed. Why do minister's children go astray? Could it be that their parents concentrate on sins or other evils rather than on cooperation and helpfulness? One needs to make a positive goal and work towards it.

I joined VOICES a support organization for individuals who had been sexually abused in one form or another. We were a very diverse group with every background imaginable and every type of experience that had affected us in various ways. We met regularly, sharing our stories, what helped us might help others. It was the first time I heard about multiple personality disorder and saw it manifest. Some of our gay members thought Toronto was more tolerant than Vancouver. They felt safer back East. As I had learned a lot working at Our Cabana, I learned a lot as a member of this group. I don't believe it exists anymore.

When I left Voices, I checked out WAVAW Women Against Violence Against Women but I found them too rabid, too anti,,,,,, They believed that only Japanese people should write books on Japanese culture, so it was wrong for me to write one as an observer. Well, I didn't fit their mold.

Around this time I read Carl Roger's "Man the Manipulator" and Viktor Frankl's "Man's Search for Meaning". The latter really impressed me. It is short, 143 pages of insightful writing. But, somehow I still go back to the poems by Kipling—"East is East and West is West" and "If" which are so empowering. I also, remember "Abou Ben Ahmed" these poems should be required reading for every teen-ager to discuss.

RACCOONS IN THE BACK YARD, ELLEN AND I HAVING TEA.

Dear Roxsane,   *Oct 24/90.*

Now don't fall over, boy, the promises I made to myself, tonight I'll write only to have something come up. I just don't know where the summer went. I guess you were busy, too, as you didn't write either. So you'll be a grandma again. I forgot when –Yvette did tell me, but me and my good memory.

So how are you doing? I'm sure there is something exciting going on. Here it is always the same. The boys finally got all the crop in, the baling done, weaned the calves and now are putting anhydrous in the fields. They sure can keep me going. The crops and field corn were quite good now if there was only a price for the grain.

Ashley started school and is quite thrilled with it. I can just imagine the things she tells her "Madame Pinette". I keep Travis quite often when Ashley is off to school. Joanne keeps getting called to the bank and she's also got a job with the watershed. She can do a lot of this at home though, like make up her minutes for the meetings and her many letters so she just has to go in the office to type it all out. Her first meeting was in Winnipeg at the parliament building and she had lunch with a bunch of men. Her next one is in Neepawa and in Nov 2.5 days in Brandon so she's getting around and the wages are good. Their house is coming along now—nothing too much done all summer.

Yesterday they poured the floor in the basement and the siding will be next. The cupboards are being looked after. Today the CAT was there to fill in around the house and make the lane. They'd like to move in in Dec. I bought them tickets for a week in Florida Jan. 5th. They've never been anywhere and will deserve a holiday. I wasn't going to go but they said they wouldn't go unless I go so we'll be going all 5 of us if nothing goes wrong.

I really should have been going to see Alfred, he phoned one night he was quite lonely for a while we thought of going Gerald and Cecile would have come with me but then they had his brother and wife coming from Ottawa and Cecile took sick so we'll try and go later after this other trip.-probably drive down rather than take the train. Well, guess I'll write a few more letters while I'm at it. No saying   when I'll get to it again.

How is Nancy? Is she still in Europe?
We hope to hear from you and let me know what's all going on
with you. Bye for now, Love, Marie Rose.

Chapter fifteen persons of interest
Several fellows who responded to my personal column ad.
Miro, the alcoholic tenant who rented my basement suite
Bill, the love of my life. Johnson, one of my long term homestays

CHAPTER FIFTEEN

FINDING MISTER RIGHT

You may be right I may be crazy but...5ft.2, eyes of blue, S/W/F.... read the classified ad I placed in the Sun personal column, by that time I had been single for about five years. I'd been going to singles dances since I came back from Mexico in 1987, starting with a Valentine's dance at the Hyatt, where I won a yard long box of chocolates. Yes, I went to the dance alone, but I met a few people, and had a few dances, but nothing to follow up on. I kept working, traveling when I could, and going to dances when the spirit moved me. I was looking for a serious relationship, but had no luck so I tried a personal ad—that was in 1990.

Well, I got over two dozen replies. An interesting, interested bunch. Some I read, put in a pile, and later answered with a thanks for responding, good luck in the future, but I'm sorry it won't work for me letter. That eliminated about half of them. Then I set up mini dates to meet the others. Usually that was "let's have coffee at the White Spot at 7 pm to chat.'

Most of the men, even the two doctors were too needy—too lonely— they needed someone who would entertain them, nurture them, and take over where their mothers had left off. Not for me. Life had taught me we create our own happiness, and trying to make someone else happy is draining—at times impossible. I was not going back there.

I met business men, a diabetic who insisted on going out for dinner, ordering a full meal, consuming the mound of potatoes, two slices of bread, and a beer. Then he told me he was a nudist. That was scary. He was a good twenty years older than the photo he sent, and obviously couldn't take care of himself. Another dead end.

One fellow who wrote lived in a remote community way up the coast with very little social contact. Just he and me—well, I need a good social network---unless the other person is perfect. I wasn't willing to leave my friends and relatives to check that one out. Too chicken.

Another wooed me with flowers and pearls. He was a sharp dresser with confidence, a great conversationalist. Good prospect, but about our fifth or sixth meeting it came out that he was a Muslim who already had a wife. He was kind, and sent me letters and cards for a few years. I didn't want that kind of relationship---too bad.

One of the doctors I met was a great guy, but he couldn't understand why I had in my mind that I needed to find myself a full time job that paid at least sixteen dollars an hour. For some reason I'd set the goal that I had to prove to myself I could support myself. I had to be able to stand on my own two feet first. If I'd met him later on it might have worked out as he wanted someone who would assist him on his jaunts to bring sight to people in Africa or India. That could have been a real adventure. Not ready.

But to show you how the wind was blowing I'll admit the person I spent the most time with was a younger single Dad who didn't have a steady job, was caretaker for his elementary school children, rode transit or a bike. We would meet at the Law Courts downtown, sit on the concrete walls, talk and watch the myriad mice run all over the place. Life is crazy.

Of course searching for a mate, a lifelong partner didn't end there. In about 1990 or 1991 I tried a dating service. I probably met half a dozen men. The most memorable was a logger. I forget exactly what his job was, but he was short, powerfully built, had long dark hair, a full beard and arrived on a motorcycle in full leathers—what a shock! I seem to recall he carried a hunting knife. I stayed long enough to drink my tea.

Later, I gave up really trying but I joined a fellowship group called Discovery that had singles dances every first, third, and fifth Friday nights at the Unitarian church Hall at Oak and 49th. It cost five dollars admission—no alcohol allowed, smoking only outside. At the door you were given a number from one to nine then at seven thirty you were sent off to a meeting room to discuss the topic of the day. Each group had a facilitator. Soon I became one. We would get together, explain the topic, and listen to everyone's feedback or perspective. Being a teacher with a facility to remember names it was an easy job for me. The hour flew by, and soon the buzzer would sound indicating it was dance time. We'd all head out to the hall, grab a glass of juice, tea or coffee, and start off with two or three mixer dances so everyone had a partner. After that we were on our own.

BILL ON THE LOGS

I'd been attending fairly regularly for quite some time when one evening I decided to take the alcoholic tenant who lived downstairs along to show him you could have a good time without alcohol. Somehow he turned up in my group; tried to monopolize the conversation on how to deal with anger, and made the evening challenging. A new fellow—tall, confident with sparkly eyes full of curiosity was, also, part of the group.

It was obvious to the group that I knew the downstairs tenant. When the buzzer went off we went to the dance floor. I didn't pay much attention to M. after that as he made himself scarce during the dance. After the mixers I noticed the new fellow. He reminded me of a stag looking out over the field. He was nursing a glass of juice. I went up, and asked him to dance. He couldn't turn me down. We danced together two or three times that evening. I danced with several other fellows in between. At the end we both went our own ways. I collected M. and headed home.

Two weeks later I went alone. It was best. Oh, the tall fellow came back, and we spent more time together. At the end of the evening he offered to take me home, but I had my own car. He asked for my home phone number, and we became better acquainted going to the dances, the swap meet—I bought an Eswing hammer, and a small carpenter's plane. We met in August. It took till November 25th, 1992 to get a kiss. That night he'd come for dinner. Johnson, my Taiwanese homestay student, had lit a fire in the fireplace, and quietly vanished to his room to study. Now 26 years later we both remember Johnson's efforts to get us together .

BILL AND I ON GROUSE MOUNTAIN

Chapter sixteen persons of interest

Paul, Fran and Omer's son-my Godson Ray and his fiancée,Susan

Shirley and Ian Cooke's family former student Anne Chen

Homestay students Minoru, Katsutoshi, James, Kazunari, Shigenori, Tony, Masahiro, Goichi, Vincent, Johnson, Frank, Ruby, Vivian, Hedy, Deborah, Vin, Billy, Yvette, her children-Randi and Kori Nancy

The Parthenay family-MarieRose, Denis and Gilles: Diane- Vincent's cousin John, the construction foreman, the plumber Al, and Don the handyman

CHAPTER SIXTEEN

HOMESTAY STUDENTS

Since I am the eldest of seven children I am comfortable sharing my home with guests both short and long term. When the chance came up to host paying foreign students and to mentor them I was glad of the income and the company. The first two came from Dorset, a private College near City Hall in Vancouver. Minoru and Katsutoshi were two young Japanese fellows with working holiday visas. Dorset offered an eight week Introductory English program and found their students suitable homestay places. I was responsible for showing them how to get around in Greater Vancouver; how the banking system and transit systems worked; and to help them find a job. Katsu bought an older model Toyota Celica. His Dad had a friend in the fishing industry so his job was already arranged.

Paul, my Godson who came by often, teased him about his silly car. Paul, Katsu and Minoru got along with my downstairs tenant, Ray. Ray, you will remember had full blown Tourette's. At this time he was often out with his fiancée, Susan. They were planning a Spring wedding.

Minoru worked in a lab that perfected cake icings and such but when winter was approaching Whistler's ski hills beckoned. In Japan he could be a ski instructor but his limited English made that impossible here. However, he got a job running a snow grooming machine. As I had no TV at the time they offered to pay for the monthly cable bill if I bought a TV. I did. I took these fellows to Minter Gardens, all around Greater Vancouver and even to my friends' Christmas dinner in Chilliwack. Minoru and I keep in touch every Christmas so I know his families activities in Hokkaido, Japan. Here is the last letter Katsu sent me in 1990. I found this letter the other day and must say I'm impressed with his ability to use English effectively. Katsu is like my brother, Ross—good, caring, and helpful when you are in the same city. Otherwise he is busy living life wherever he is so no contact from afar.

Hi! How are you doing? Roxsane today I arrived Los Angeles.
I had a lot of interesting experience and some bad experience
I arrived New York on January 21st at night and found a cheap
Hotel and put my bag in my room and then I went out about
Ten o'clock walking around Broadway when I walked on very
Narrow road somebody touch [hit]? My shoulder there was
Two blackman one blackman had a plastic bag but he dropped
And he said it was my fault in a bag there is broken liquor bottle
[I think it's already broken] and I said I'm sorry [I should not
say so} blackman said"I bought it today and I payed $40 for
this liquor, it's your fault give me $40. And I said "do you have
a receipt? But he has a perfect receipt and I said "I don't have
$40 I have 30 Canadian dollers, finaly he discount "ok. Give
me $10.Fortunately there is a police woman and I said there is
a policeman over there come on come with me,as I said so they
escaped into darkness they are called ATARIYA. ATARI means
touch Ya means men new York's atariya is very famous between
Japanese because they always aim rich [looks rich?] Japanese who
can't speak English. It was a bad experience in new York but I
think New York is one of the most exciting city in the world. Times
squer broadway and I will never forget night vieaw from Brooklyn
Bridge and Empire State Bldg.
Are you busy? How's everything going? Is anybody come to your
house to stay your house? How is Ray? How is Paul? I really miss
you some day I want meet you in Japan[maybe in Canada].
I will send a letter sometime. See you later.

This letter is enough to make any teacher proud. Put yourself in his shoes. He is in a foreign country with a totally different alphabet/ character system yet he is getting across exactly what he wants to say.

When Minoru and Katsutoshi left, Shigenori and Kazunari came. I began teaching at Dorset College in Vancouver in January 1990. I taught English as a Second Language; Canadian History and Art. I drove Shige and Kaz back and forth, too.

Kaz was still searching for a better job as the semester ended.. He wanted to try in Banff so we went there en route to visit Yvette and family in Portage la Prairie, Manitoba. It was April and the temperature was in the thirties when we arrived. Yvette soon got us busy planting Saskatoon bushes. Two days later we woke up to eighteen inches of snow.

Yvette's father-in-law was suffering with bone cancer. As a person with a strong belief in being able to die rather than suffer through again and again, I explained my feelings to his wife. I was glad when he was checked into the hospital. He died while we were there. I was surprised when Kaz pulled his dress suit out of his luggage so he would be properly dressed for the funeral. We went to the funeral.

After that we went to Ste. Rose du Lac where Denis and Gilles Parthenay—MarieRose's sons, were still delivering calves many nights. Kaz was awe-struck. I don't think he had been on a farm before. The cattle, the huge equipment, the size of the fields, all were foreign to him. On our way back I left him in Banff to work for the summer. Shige had gone back to Japan to complete his studies.

Dear Roxsanne
How are you? I'm fine
I found job. It is Banff International Hotel.
My job is house keeping, every day, clearing only. [$6/hr]
I found job after your back home soon.
Accomodationis very small 4 dollors a day.
I working 7-8 hours a day.
Maybe I will not much saving money.
This job I will work Hotel is many Japanese penpal.
I not use English. I will be not good speak English well.
B y the way If your house and Yvette house come little for me.
Please sending littler.
Mail Address Gen. Del. Banff AB T0L 0C0
Accomodition Address #B7 512 Banff Ave AB phone 403 762 8691 K

RUBY AND FRANK WITH MARCIA top
JOY, ?, HEDY, RUBY at bottom

Next came Tony and a Korean, who at twenty-eight, was addicted to alcohol and gambling. At the end of the month he and I agreed he should leave.

Then Masahiro came very formally dressed in his three-piece suit. It took him awhile to learn to relax. He found himself a job in a shop near Burrard Skytrain Station that sold souvenirs to Japanese tourists. His English grew slowly. Both Masa and James expected Tony to show them more respect as they were older. Tony was a much freer spirit, not really bound by convention. At this point I had yet to learn that in both Japanese and Korean cultures you must show deference—respect to anyone who is older than you even if it is only by a few weeks. Understanding this cultural difference helped me deal with other students' sensitivities when they cropped up.

While Masa was here, if I was outside and the phone rang Masa would answer it. He said he was my secretary dog. Having homestays made me want the kitchen enlarged, an en suite bath for me and a bedroom with space for a computer and desk. I started to remodel my house using plans designed by my daughter, Yvette. I added two hundred and fifty square feet across the back adding nine feet to my bedroom, an en suite with a double Jacuzzi and five feet across the kitchen.

I decided on a crawl space rather than a basement. I had to remove the soil so the foundation could be framed and the concrete poured. I decided to fill 13 wheelbarrows full every day and pile it in the corner away from the house. Soon I had quite a pile there. One Sunday morning I was busy filling the wheelbarrow when Masa came out. He couldn't believe his eyes. "Ikenai" "Ikenai!' he shouted. "That is a Japanese man's job ." But I just kept on filling the wheelbarrow. Both Masa and Ray, the downstairs tenant, helped out and we got it done.

GOICHI

When Tony moved out, Masa asked, "Can my friend. Goichi move in?" Goichi came, bringing his rice cooker, electric frying pan and sofa bed. We were a very cooperative bunch. In April, Goichi, Masa and I travelled to Portage la Prairie. We stayed in a youth hostel near Lake Louise that was very primitive-no electricity and only outdoor toilets. That was quite an experience for my city boys. While I was driving through to Portage, I tried to get them aware of life on farms of a section [six hundred and forty acres] or more. Telling them I was making a cake and ran out of sugar. Would they be able to go borrow some from the neighbours? I tried telling them we had no more room for newcomers, just to see what their comments would be.

It was Dorset College's semester break. Some days the Spring air was cool. Goichi took the train from Portage to Toronto. He wanted to see Niagara Falls as they are famous world-wide. We met his return train a week or so later. Soon we headed back to BC. I had thoroughly enjoyed my time with my daughter and grandchildren, especially getting to know Randi better. I think Kori put rocks in my hubcaps that time. What a racket until Allen took them out.

I had just finished explaining to Masa that I didn't like him telling Goichi to tell me everything. He should work on his English or he would be walking home. But as we pulled out of the driveway, he asked Goichi to tell me--- "O sashiburi" I stopped the car. I was furious but Goichi tried to explain----"O sashiburi---was I lonesome for Yvette and her family already?" I calmed down but I asked again if Masa would please talk to me directly as I could ask Goichi to translate if necessary. We agreed and headed off much more soberly but the communication improved. I don't recall where we stayed overnight but it wasn't the hostel near Lake Louise.

When we arrived home we could see the addition to the house was coming along. The plumber from Chilliwack suggested his friend John would be a good foreman as he knew construction well. John hired a labourer to help him. They framed forms for the concrete foundation; they passed inspection. He continued with the framing; had the rough plumbing installed and the electrical. Every thing was done to code. It was all ready for the roof addition to be added. The laminate beam to support the weight was in place but John was stalling. I had to be clear, firm.

There was no reason not to go ahead. It happened that semester break came that weekend so I'd be home to make sure the work would get done. John and Don removed the shingles from the existing roof. After six weeks of glorious sunshine now the interior was vulnerable. John and the plumber are Seventh Day Adventists so they quit work early on Friday. On Saturday at about eleven am there was a sudden downpour right into the kitchen, bath and bedroom. The rafters were still there but the shiplap, tarpaper, and shingles had been removed. There was a gaping hole all along the west side of the house. There was nothing to stop the water that ran down the slope of the roof so the interior was vulnerable.

I phoned Nancy. She would know what to do. She had worked on several building projects. She was studying Architecture at UBC but she was out. Drat! I tried to figure out who else might be able to help. Fifteen or twenty minutes later the rain stopped so I left a new message—not to worry. An hour and a half later the downpour returned with a vengeance. Oh my God--- water was running down the light fixtures into the kitchen. This time Nancy gave instructions:-"get the ladders, tarps, roofing nails, and slats to hold the tarps down."

"I'll be there as soon as I can." She was. And the two of us got the tarps up and the interior protected. She was a Godsend—calm, cool, capable and practical. On Monday, I discovered John's problem. He could put on a roof that rose four inches per foot but his Math was stuck because this roof rose four and a half inches per foot. When I explained to him that meant a rise of nine inches over two feet the roof went on.

About that time I was wondering if I had enough funds to get the whole thing finished. I let John go. Don and I put a new roof on the whole house before I went back to teaching. Don put on the vinyl siding.

RANDI AND MARCIA;   KORI AND MATTHEW

Yvette, and her children Randi, and Kori came out to visit .Yvette and I with the help of Randi, who at three could just carry the glass blocks, put in the exterior wall around the Jacuzzi. We replaced the old bathroom window with glass blocks and put up a small panel of them by the kitchen door. Yvette had drawn up the plans for the addition. I didn't credit her when I entered the remodelling contest as I wasn't sure you could use a professional designer. That is a decision I continue to regret. I didn't mean to be unfair to her. I just assumed in a contest everything would need to be original or something like that. I should have asked what were the exact rules. I needed a better explanation.

In the end, her plans helped us win First Prize in the Canadian Homes renovation contest. We didn't win the overall category. That went to a much larger, more elegant project designed by other professionals.. Our prize was $1200 worth of Elgar plumbing—strange—what would I need with plumbing fixtures after just remodelling my house? The prize was a bathtub, [sold to my sister]; two vanity sinks [one still not used the other in our main bathroom]; a toilet [sold to my sister] and two sets of faucets.

At the same time as the first contest there was another contest for bedroom window treatments. My black soutache braid on white pellon fake Japanese shoji coverings won first prize. We now have a Dufferin Games Room solid oak brass trimmed bar, still in its box, in the basement. I'd much rather have had the second prize, a set of tools.

The magazine sent a professional out to photograph the kitchen and bedroom. The Ikea white kitchen cabinets and the glass front upper and lower storage unit complimented the faux black granite counter tops and island surface. We added bright red Guatemalan placemats, white china and stainless cutlery for effect.

PRIZE WINNING KITCHEN

Masa and Goichi were very good companions. Both tried to help whenever they could. Goichi has a great sense of humour. He bought me a squawking chicken toy once and a very cosy après-ski jacket with snowmen all over it. I often called Goichi "51 Kobayashi" as in Japanese 'go'is five and 'ichi 'is one. Goichi loved to cook, too. He taught me how to make Ishikari nabe a fish stew popular in Hokkaido. We made a great family.

At Christmas Masa stayed home while Nancy and I went to Mexico. Goichi came with us as far as Los Angeles but went on to check out Guatemala City and Belize. Nancy and I probably stopped to visit Cousin Sarah, Don and Nicole in California; then continued on to Our Cabana, one of Guiding's World Centers, where I used to be Program Director, in Cuernavaca, Mexico. Later we met my Godson, Paul in Mexico City. He had begun his holiday in Ixtapa-Zihuatenejo but continued on with us to Palenque in Chiapas. The ruins there are outstanding.

NANCY AT PALENQUE

I was fascinated by the codicils telling the history of the Mayan people. Nancy was impressed with the architecture and Paul was busy taking photographs of us at every turn. I remember on my guided tour of Tikal [in Guatemala] the tour guide pointed out the Aztec pyramid situated prominently amid the Mayan ones. International experiences and relationships have been with us a very long time.

While at Our Cabana I was pleasantly surprised to find almost all of the recommendations I had made in December 1987 had been put in place by December 1991. I was, also, surprised to find which of the staff had stood by me and which had not.

From Our Cabana we went to Oaxaca where I purchased a small tapestry in a design attributed to Escher where the birds became fish or vice versa. Nancy bought a piece of intricately patterned black pottery, a regional speciality. Oaxaca with its pottery, woven goods and in early

January its home-made, artisan created hot air balloon contest has always had a special attraction for me.

The ruins of Mitla and Monte Alban are examples from past cultures that leave one full of awe. How were these constructions possible? Who designed them? Why here? The perfection, the precision and their purpose lead to many more questions. Were the designs at Monte Alban from cadavers? from an early medical culture or a shamanistic retreat? The designs I remember are of a pregnancy of twins; a breach birth and other medical emergencies. They are definitely not of dancers as the tour guide tried to tell us.

Paul flew back to Vancouver from Mexico City. I think he was most impressed with his accommodation in Ixtapa-Zihuatenejo. I'll never forget Palenque and the huge Olmec sculptures and cages made of stone in the park in Villahermosa or the long taxi ride from Palenque to the airport.

When Masa returned to Japan he wore his three-piece suit and instantly became Japanese---reserved. Goichi left around the same time leaving us the rice cooker, the electric frying pan, the sofa bed. They both left many great memories.

When Goichi left I had been teaching at NWSS for more than a year. My ESL class was used to frequent reports of the homestay students and I; our adventures, misunderstandings and cultural adaptations. So, I sadly told them how I would miss Goichi and Masa. Up to this point my homestays had come through Dorset College. They were all young adults 22 to 28 years old here on two year working holiday visas.

RUBY AND MARCIA   JOHNSON AND MARCIA

My next homestay student, the first from Taiwan came through Anne Chen's friendship with Diane, a cousin of Vincent Sung. Mr. Sung was hoping for a place for Vincent who had registered at NWSS. Johnson moved in about the same time as Vincent. He had requested moving in in his journal assignment the day I told the class Goichi and Masa were going home. Frank's request came soon after that.

Johnson, a meticulous, polite, very conservative Taiwanese, individual was almost the opposite of affable, sturdy Vincent. Vincent is an out going, people person much like his father. He enjoyed being at NWSS as there were several other Taiwanese students. Soon they put together a hockey team. Bill took the boys to Squamish to climb the Chief, a real challenge. We went many places as a family.

One summer Johnson, Anne Chen and I went camping. We packed the tent, a portable stove, pots and pans, cutlery, dishes, sleeping bags and all. We headed out early eager to try something new. We had a snack at Hope, drove on to Cache Creek where I had a Rueben Sandwich for lunch. Maybe it was too late a lunch for me or maybe I was just tense. Anyway I started to develop a migraine headache. By the time we reached Quesnel and found a campsite I pulled in, stopped, got out and tossed out the tent, pegs and all, plus the stove and groceries and told them I was taking my pills and going to sleep. And I did.

CAMPING WITH ANNE AND JOHNSON

Fortunately they got the tent up, the stove working and supper was ready very quickly. I don't think either of them had been camping before. When I told the other teachers they were impressed with how well Anne and Johnson had done. The next morning my headache was gone. Maybe we drove to Barkerville, I can't quite remember but we spent the next night at Marisa's, a friend of mine, in Prince George. We were off after breakfast on our way to McBride and Edmonton. We checked out the Mall then headed south. Our destination was Drumheller and the Dinosaur Museum. We weren't in a rush so we poked around a couple of small towns when I needed a break from driving or something special came up. We really enjoyed the Tyrell Dinosaur Museum leaving just after a late supper heading west.

It was too wet to camp so we drove on in the dark seeking a motel when all of a sudden I tried to stop but hit the barricade just hard enough to knock it over. The map showed the road went straight through but for whatever reason, it was closed off. The car wasn't damaged. None of us were hurt. There weren't any warning signs. We put the barricade back up and headed north. An hour later someone spotted the motel sign so we turned in for the night. We returned through Calgary and Banff. We were gone five or six days. We had a good time and were ready to go back to school.

Shortly after that Anne went back to Taiwan to spend time with her family. Later she registered at the College at Shoreline near Seattle. When she graduated from Washington State Bill and I attended the ceremony in Pullman, Washington. Anne was never a homestay in my house but she was my student in 1990 and became a lifelong friend.

Johnson stayed with us for five years. From high school where I knew he could pass the TOEFL test and get a higher mark than most high school seniors, he went on to Douglas College where he worked on the college newspaper but progressed slowly as if he was carrying a burden. Maybe that burden was his mother who phoned at 8:30 most Saturday mornings and told him he should be studying, told him not to go to parties, to work at getting good grades. Most of us don't cope well with this kind of advice.

Johnson often made me shake my head. He wanted to know what was the difference between "happy" and "glad". When I commented that he used the same table cleaning technique as did the staff at Our Cabana in Mexico he asked years later, "Do you know why they used that technique?" He needed a reason for everything. When he finally got to UBC studying psychology he figured out he is a perfectionist. Like my father his need for perfectionism slows him down or stops him from achieving all that he could. Johnson could take more than two hours to eat his supper. He kept every newspaper that he hadn't found the time to read entirely so the stack in his room was almost four feet high when he moved. He is a kind, wonderful person who often proceeds at a snail's pace.

Vincent went on to Douglas College. He focused on Economics gathering information that would help him in international commerce. Both Johnson and Vincent are back in Taiwan. Both would rather live here.

Frank was the next homestay. Ruby who has since changed her name to Jenny came a few months after him. Frank at fifteen was someone his parents trusted to collect the mail from his uncle's house when his uncle went back to Taiwan, to see the utilities and municipal taxes were paid. He was reliable, responsible, creative and had a great sense of humour. Ruby was tiny, artistic and out going. The pair of them became close friends. Each one reminded the other of whatever they needed to do next. Either of them could fix and deliver tea to the other.

MIKE LOI AND STUDENTS AT NWSS.

They had a large circle of friends and we thought they were so happy together but someone behind the scenes didn't want that to be permanent. Whoever it was fed poisonous information to Ruby's Mom. That led to them going their separate ways. Both Ruby and Frank had their own cars. Both of them went to University of the Fraser Valley. Ruby studied Fine Art. Frank studied business. Ruby now Jenny is in Taiwan happily married with a two year old daughter. Frank is successful, happily married with two charming little boys Sanders and Cheung. Frank and Joey met me when I was in Hong Kong in 2014. His wife, Joey, his Mom, Frank and the boys took me and a friend of mine, Mila, for dim sum and then to do a little shopping.

I stayed with Jenny in Taipei en route to Motoko's in 2016. Staying in Taipei en route to seeing Motoko gives me a chance to touch base with many of my ex-students. We get together for lunch or supper depending on my flight schedule. Johnson always takes off time from work to show me the highlights. I usually see Tony Yang, Vincent, Johnson and LiWen, too.

JESSICA, ROXSANE AND HEDY

After Vincent left, Hedy moved in. She was quiet, but had a bubbly sense of humour. She applied herself to learning English and shared her room with her sister Deborah who settled in just before I went to Asia marketing. Deborah was very shy so while I was away she kept a low profile. A couple of years back she came to visit with her even shyer husband and little Lucien. Lucien is the opposite to his parents—free as a breeze, friendly with everyone, living life to the fullest. Deborah came to apologize to Bill for not coming out for dinner when I was away. She gave him a big hug and tears rolled down her face. She knew he was kind. We were both surprised. It was good to see her again. She runs an English pre-school in Taiwan, I believe. Both Hedy and Deborah moved to share an apartment with their younger sister Nicole when she was accepted in NWSS.

BILLY AND VIN

The last pair of students were Vin and Billy. They were brother and sister. Billy was the younger. He would stay up half the night visiting his friends in Taiwan on ICHAT. Then it was extremely difficult to get him up and to school. This constant battle was wearing. I was not prepared for Vin to not come home after school on the Thursday before Easter. Her mom's friend phoned on Good Friday so I told her I had not seen Vin since Thursday morning when I took her to school. I was not only concerned but getting angry at her lack of consideration.

I phoned her Mom and she said everything would be all right but I said NO, when she goes home for the summer that is it. They cannot come back. Vin didn't show up till sometime Monday. I'm sure I explained why I was upset clearly and emphatically. I had no trouble with her after that. But I was surprised when in June she said "See you in September". I said "No, I told your Mom you can not come back." Apparently her Mom didn't want to believe that. I hear from Vin once in a while. Maybe her Easter absence was a turning point for her.

That was all of our homestay students but we had a request for lodging for a teacher from Japan who had been invited to help out our Japanese teacher. I'm not sure, I just understood she was here and not getting paid. We agreed to put her up for $300 a month but then inflation hit so I asked for fifty dollars more and though that barely covered costs she said, " no way". You can imagine how surprised I was when just before she went back to Japan she went down to Robson Street and bought herself a $1300 Feragamo bag. She is a vibrant, attractive young woman, trained to be a teacher but she much prefers to be a travel guide or a stewardess. She is always on the go. Sometimes there is a romantic angle to play out but as they say a rolling stone gathers no moss. Her Canadian mail still comes here but I only see her every few years.

Dear Roxsane and Bill,
Again my daughter is visiting you.
She likes you and the surroundings very much.
As you know, she is such a girl who cannot stop to think, please give her your clever advice.
I wish you a Merry Christmas and a happy new year!
With Love, A. Y.

Bill and I prefer to have our house to ourselves now. We like to have room for our guests.

BILL AND MR. AND MRS. LIAO—RUBY'S PARENTS

Dear Gradma

guess what yestrday
we made crsmis
decrashins. We made them 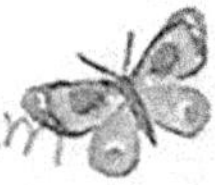
with spisise. Do you noe why?
because they are spis
decrashins. And remeber I
will olwys love you. I
can't whate in till ante Nansy
and ukll Gord gets here.

Love Randi

TRACY CHAN top   SERVING GIRLS AT LOTTE

Chapter seventeen persons of interest
Tracy Chan, a former student Tony Lam, now like an adopted son
Wan Lin, a Taiwanese tourist in Hong Kong
Mal McLeod, an ESL teacher at Dorset College.

CHAPTER SEVENTEEN

1991 SEMESTER BREAK

At semester break in the summer of 1991 I went to Korea and Hong Kong. In Korea I stayed in a yogwan [like a hostel], near Ulchiro-Ilgo station in Seoul. Tracy Chan, a student of mine, met me and took me out to see the Korean Folk Museum, a spacious complex featuring many facets of time gone by. The next few days another guest and I explored the local area. There was a Lotte [Japanese Department Store], nearby, so we went to their restaurant floor to choose our meals each day. There were many, many choices. We couldn't read the Korean labels, but we looked at the plastic food in the display cases and noted their prices. Soon I was flying into Hong Kong.

I stayed in the Youth Hostel on Victoria Hill taking the Metro link to Kennedy Station, and hiking in the rest of the way. I met a couple of characters there…During the day I went into Hong Kong or Kowloon checking out the bird market; the gem market; and various parts of town. I went to Aberdeen, to Sim Chat Sui and more.

Tony Lam was staying there. I never did figure out why. But, he offered to be my tour guide—of course, I accepted. He was amiable, a young fellow working in the currency exchange. He had lived in Hong Kong all his life. He knew every nook and cranny well. He took two or three of us around the first day, using the Metro. Then as we became better acquainted one day we went to a taxi stand where he worked on occasion, and borrowed a taxi for the day. I was amazed. We went out to the New Territories, right to the border of Communist China. I saw the small towns, the markets, the whole works. On one of the last days he suggested to Wan Lin, a Taiwanese woman, and I that we take the Aquacat to Macau. What a day. A boat excursion on a sunny day is so enjoyable. We got off and explored Macau on foot. Tony was twenty-seven years old; Wan Lin in her late twenties/early thirties, and I was fifty-one. As we went up and down the streets, Wan Lin translated Chinese to me, Tony pointed out historical sites, and I translated any Spanish or French. I remember quincaillerie—a hardware store…After a day of tromping up and down we came to a Dragon Museum—maybe dinosaurs—I thought. Wan Lin was tired out. She was becoming the tail of the dragon. I am sure each of us slept well that night. Before I caught the plane home Tony and I had become good friends, so I invited him to come visit me in Canada.

A few days after I came back I stopped into Dorset College to chat with the principal. "Roxsane—I'm so sorry. We have bad news. Our registration is way down. We have no job for you." I was tenth from the bottom of the list when I went on holiday, but after the car accident that Ada died in, the Hong Kong registration fell from 450 to 276. It wasn't the college's fault. The two of them were headed to Whistler to watch the sunrise when the driver crashed into a rock wall. She wasn't wearing a seatbelt. She was thrown from the car and died.

In the next breath, the principal said, "Mal came in yesterday, and said there is an opening in the International Section of New Westminster Secondary for another English As a second Language instructor. You should apply." I got my resume in by two o'clock. The interview was at eight pm, and the job was mine. The salary was better, too.

Dear Roxsane,

How are you doing in those days? I haven't heard from you & write to you for a long long time. In this long time there were several things happened to me

I started working in school for almost a month. I work as cashier & coffee maker in Cub [it is like a cafeteria] It's fun & new experiences for me. I face different people + things everyday but it becomes kind of heavy job for me now since I have lots of assignments + reading to do.

Last two weeks, I got a friend passed away on the road to Pullman during the car accident. It's very sad since he was a really nice person. I enjoy to have him as friend. Because this accident, I meet a nice guy whose name is David. There are so many similarity between us. It's so comfortable to be with him. He is my boyfriend now which is only two weeks from now. I was pretty surprise since we only know each other for one week before we become a couple. He is so nice+ and care about me a lot. I felt in love this time. We talk about our future sometimes. He was born in Taiwan but grew up in Hong Kong which mean his family is in Hong Kong. We feel bad about the separation after the graduation. He says he will go back to Taiwan for living later. Maybe it's too early to talk about this right now. I don't know how long I will be go with him since the longest time to have a boyfriend is only a couple of months.

How is thing going for you? Since I haven't heard from you I guess you are doing good +busy for your life. How is Bill, Frank, Vincent? I heard you got a girl as homestay student, isn't it? Surprise! Surprise! Is she becoming Frank's girlfriend?

God! I have three exam this week and two homework assignments due tomorrow so I had better stop right here! Take care yourself, Roxsane. Say Hello to everybody for me, thank you.

Love, Anne 9:50 am WSU

Hi! How are you doing after while? Are you still noisy in the house, Get out there. That's my house! Anyway when I arrived in Narita Airport I met my friends whose Satoko, Naoko we had talked in our future or our having job.and then I was checked out in my bags what inside the police suspect. I was little worried about my two books which I brought from Canada such as nude books, 2,3 minutes later the police found out those books, whose very upset. I thought this is scally staff but I thought 'shit". Much later I arrived at Chitoce Airport. My friend waited for me. I was very impressed. Now I still having culture shock. I am very grad to meet my friends, my parents but my feeling not getting happy even Japanese foods triffick or bar. Singing Karaoke. What my thought is people are "smoked' which I can't stand especially many girls smoke not care of other people whose not smoking and people are not friendly, nasty things people talked about like I studied in Canada without working. You just used up parents money that's nothing meaning. Nobody understand me. I think just Satoko, Naoko, Toshi, Masa whose we are studied with together understand me before two days my Dad came back from Tokyo, we took family meeting our future. I honestly said to my Dad "I think that if I would like to take a job in Japan as soon as I will be get. But what my feeling is don't want to working in Japan. I want to try to job in Canada and then my dad said he doessn't want to my mam only her in my house so that he decided he's going to quit the job. Coming back to the house in December that I have to stay in my house until December. When I lived in Canada I very respect my motherland very proud of but now I am not. I think tomorrow apply to working holiday Visa in Tokyo while I apply I gotta be take part time job I don't know what kind job, but I have to make money for going to Vancouver. After my Dad he will come back to my house he might have new job in here. I think that no problem. My Dad agreed with that. My mam little worried about I'm always talk other friend what do I have to do but it is not going to be solved.

I am very miss you. I need your help I can't swim without you. Please write me a letter what can I do that!! From problem child, G

Adios Amigo.

ESL TEACHERS AT HALLOWE'EN

Chapter eighteen persons of interest
ESL teachers at New Westminster Secondary Mike Loi, student liason

CHAPTER EIGHTEEN

TEACHING AT NEW WESTMINSTER SECONDARY HIGH SCHOOL

I had the class that struggled with English. They were intelligent enough. Most of them did well in Math or the Sciences, but English was a real hurdle. The five other teachers tried to help me, but it was a tough assignment. All of the students wanted into regular high school classes. How would they survive? At the end of the term I set them up for testing at VCC's King Edward campus. I didn't know the previous teacher had done the same, and promised they'd never have to take that test again. In the end we passed the brightest ones, and were amazed when they succeeded.

After that I decided that the students would learn better if the language lessons had specific content, so we bought a set of texts from Fitzhenry Whiteside CANADA, GROWTH OF A NATION. I followed the pattern used by a Social Studies teacher I had met at North Delta when I was tutoring Glen. Using this method their English grew. They learned about Canada-first the provinces and their capitals. Then the physical geography; followed by the economic geography; then the First Nations, the Explorers and our history. This gave them a good basis for citizenship if they stayed in Canada. It gave them an understanding of our government and laws if they returned home to foster international trade. It, also, covered Grade Ten Social Studies and prepared them for Grade Eleven.

LUCIE, SHERRY, LORI, RALPH AND ROSE MUSIC FOR ALL.

The International program worked separately from the regular high school, but we were in the same building complex. We had our own office with a secretary, homestay coordinator, marketing team, high school liason, and principal/department head. The six teachers got together for lunch often. We planned joint activities—field trips, holiday celebrations, and shared general insights. We had a great program, and an amazingly dedicated staff that poured their hearts into their jobs. They really did their utmost to empower their students to become the best citizens they could by promoting cross cultural understanding.

One morning when I was teaching in NWSS before we settled in for Home Room there was a PA announcement that there had been a call saying there was a bomb in the school. The message was short and specific—send the students home. They were to get away from the school—no one was to hang around. Once our classrooms were clear the teachers were to assemble in the Library-really?- Once all were there we were told we must go back to our classroom and check every desk for possible explosives! REALLY! Can you imagine the state of my friend who had been a child in Holland during WWII. I simply volunteered to check out her classroom, too. She needed to go home. Was there no one with common sense in control?

DAN, ROSE, AND LUCIE MUSIC TO RELAX BY.

Another time a group of upset young fellows stormed through the halls smashing things as they went. Not all of them were from our school. Yes, they seemed to be of a specific ethnic group. Again, shut your classroom doors. Counsel students leaving to go straight home in pairs if possible. No-it was not racist but one fellow whose ex-girlfriend was dating someone in a different group got his group out to help him express his displeasure. I'm not sure what the follow up was. Whatever it was a well-kept secret. Thank God our students don't usually pack knives or guns.

The school district wanted the money that came in from the foreign students, and someone decided that money would be better used if the International Section was absorbed by the regular high school. After all, they had English as a Second Language classes for immigrants. At first both the High School staff and the International staff fought the proposed change. We had separate union representation but eventually we were swallowed up by the high school. In order to do this we were forced to teach some regular high school classes. Most ended up teaching English. The classes were larger, the discipline generally poorer. But, the pay was better, and our pensions were guaranteed. I became part of the Social Studies Department, sometimes part of the Home Economics Department, and later on part of the Art Department. At times I taught Grade 11 Socials; often I taught a class in Career and Personal Planning; once I taught Textile Arts and Crafts. We had to fit in where the need was and I could. I continued this way until I retired in 2003.

?, VERA AND MR.TURTLTAUB IN SEOUL

Chapter nineteen persons of interest
Bill who cared for my homestays while I was away
Mr. Turtletaub, a teacher from Dorset College
Vera, an instructor at Thompson Rivers University
Johnson's Mom and Dad
Vincent Sung's Dad and cousin, Diane
My sister, the Mayor
Motoko, Kuniko, Kikue my friends
Po,Thomas, Derek, students in the car crash
Jerry and Kenneth Yeh

CHAPTER NINETEEN

MARKETING IN ASIA 1993

Recruiting new students involved traveling abroad. In late1992 the International section wanted to send a representative to the February/ March educational marketing fairs in Asia sponsored by the BC Government. I was the only one willing to go alone., but I couldn't go and leave my homestay students on their own.

When I explained to Bill that I could not leave my students he offered, to look after them for me. He would see that they had breakfast, make their supper, and deal with anything that came up. The students thought that was fine. And, just before I left they asked if their friend, Vivian, could stay for a month while her Mom went back to Taiwan. I told her Mom Bill was going to look after the students, but she was determined to have Vivian stay so Bill ended up with five students in his care.

The International section ordered the flights, arranged the hotels and even a special translator for Taipei. I agreed to stop in Moriguchi, Japan to bring greetings from the City of New Westminster. My sister was the Mayor of New Westminster at the time. I was to meet a few Japanese parents as well.

I was surprised to find that the posh Westin Chosun Hotel where I stayed in Seoul was only a block away from the yogwan I had stayed in in 1991. I had taken high heels to make a good impression, but soon realized that I needed flat shoes. I got excellent advice from the ambassador's wife during one of our conversations. I bought the shoes that made my job so much easier. I could walk faster than the taxis could go in downtown Seoul, but finding the addresses of the Korean agents was difficult. I believe this was one of the first education fairs in Seoul.

It was opened by the Canadian Ambassador and very well attended. The representatives were taken to a special dinner in a heritage restaurant run by Monks. It was hosted by the Ambassador. Since I have several allergies I had had my Korean students write please do not feed Roxsane onions, garlic, wheat, or papaya on a business card. I gave this to the waiter who looked at me amazed. Then he went into the kitchen. He came back—-out of the sixteen courses, I could eat just two, potatoes cooked with honey, and a rice gruel.

After dinner Mr. Turtletaub, an old acquaintance from Dorset College, Vera from Thompson Rivers, and I got in a taxi following the crowd to Itaewan, the shopping area on the American military base where I think several others bought Nikes and other treasures.

During the next few days I saw agents, visited with parents, and looked after visitors to our booth. One of my jobs was to check out the Korean agents but I wasn't able to decide if one was better than the other. I needed more information.

I had dinner and a tour of the city by night courtesy of one of our student's parents. I got their daughter confused with one of my students who had the same name but I didn't figure that out until I returned. As I was leaving the hotel the desk clerk presented me with a gift—a pair of Chosen pottery ducks in a small wooden box. They were happy to have had me as a guest.

My next stop was Taipei where Johnson's father met me on the plane, walked me through customs, and took me to my hotel. That night I had supper with him and his wife. The next day I had appointments with parents, and a meeting with the young lady from BC Trade Centre who would translate for me. We went over the presentation, as well as possible questions and answers. That evening Vincent a former homestay student's Dad and his cousin toured me through the night market.

FORUM FOR Q AND A SESSION IN TAIPEI;
MR.TAI AND I [JOHNSON'S DAD]

One thing I had to deal with was the fact that BC teachers were on strike! I explained as best I could that the teachers didn't get paid while on strike, and that they still had to cover the curriculum before the year was out. I, also, explained that the students had to be attending school before the 30th of September for the district to get extra funding for ESL students. The International section had to comply with BC government policy. When I met parents over tea or Dim Sum, my minimal Chinese let me toss in comments about phone calls, work, and odds and ends that helped the relationships along.

Johnson's Dad set up a fantastic day off for me. He told me to be in the hotel lobby at 5:30am to be at the airport at 6:30, and in Haulien by 7:30. We were met on landing by a Mr. Wei, who I believe was a television host. He was our chauffeur. He had a photographer with him, too. We drove out to the precarious road that Chiang Kai Chek and his engineers built through the mountains. Very impressive.

Next we met some indigenous Taiwanese people. Then we went to a marble factory where huge blocks of marble had been carved into a tree stump with a hen and chicks, along with many, many other exquisite creations. Mr. Tai wanted to give me a marble gift. So I tried telling him friendship was enough. I didn't want things. After a while the photographer took me outside, and explained I would embarrass Mr. Tai in front of his friends if I didn't choose something. I explained first of all marble is heavy, secondly, it might break in transit. What if I have three small cloisonné cups and if Mr. Tai wanted he could bring me the lovely marble vase when he came to see his son in July.

Then, we went for lunch—-with the local police force—-we were about twenty—-the crab was perfectly presented. Then as the brandy arrived, I was taken to the local beauty salon as I had mentioned getting my hair cut when I got home. The photographer accompanied me and translated for me. When the meeting was over we got back on the plane for Taipei. For sure, I had to phone Bill that night. What an adventure.

Between Johnson's Dad [and Mom] who took me through the museum, and Vincent's Dad and cousin getting all my photos printed I was treated like royalty.

Hong Kong was next. I saw several parents as arranged by our agent there. One in particular stood out. I remember his son always being late for class. His father was very late, too. In my free time I met Tony Lam, and talked about him possibly coming to Canada.

TONY LAM;   FLORA EXPO IN MORIGUCHI

After the education fair in Korea I didn't cross paths with Mr. T. or Vera again. From Hong Kong, I flew into Osaka where I met one student's parents before going to Moriguchi on behalf of the City of New Westminster. In Moriguchi I met several officials, and toured the Floral Expo with them. They kept asking if my sister, New Westminster's mayor was older than I. I assured them that wasn't the case. In Japan the oldest often gets special treatment. My sister was a very capable mayor; astute and caring. Touring the Expo my horticultural knowledge was appreciated as was the humour I could inject. I had tea with the group hosting me and made contacts that we maintained for many years. Then I was off to see the rest of the parents on my list. I met the physicist whose wife ran a ballet school. Their eldest son loved baseball and Art. He has become a well-respected San Francisco artist famous for his paintings of ballerinas.

I made my way by Shinkansen to Tokyo; then took the Odakyu line to Chofushi to see my friends Motoko, Kinuko, and Kikue briefly before returning home. Of course, all the time I was away I was in contact with Bill every few days, and with the International office as necessary.

The office required a written report on my return. I shared some of the gifts I'd received with the others, and got back to teaching. Bill had done such a good job with the homestay students that they didn't miss me at all.

Earlier that year one Monday morning in late January, Mike, the Student Liason, met me before class telling me, "Three of your students were involved in a fatal car accident yesterday. Thomas is dead. The others are in serious condition in Vancouver General Hospital."

I learned more details from the other teachers at lunch time. Po had a new car. They had been snowboarding. They dropped off another student a block or two earlier, when maybe the driver decided to pass a bus on the icy road. There was a collision and the loose snowboard hit the occupants in the head—whatever—that was what I was told.

That night I asked Bill to accompany me walking and walking to get rid of my stress. As soon as school was out the next day I drove to VGH to check on the boys. Their recovery took a long time. But they were never the same. The driver was still in a wheelchair when I saw him years later. Derek went back to his family in Taiwan. We kept in touch for a while. The International section planted a tree in Thomas's memory. He had been the only son of a top military official.

Another time that Spring Mike met me early in the morning he told me, "There has been a terrible house fire in Taipei. Jerry and Kenneth's family all died except the grandfather who was away playing cards. The boys uncle has decided they should come to school as sitting at home would probably be worse. Look after them as best you can." We did, and I took flowers to the Uncle's house as well. This was a star-crossed family.

Later on when Jerry was in his final year at UBC Kenneth needed hospitalized as he had a rare blood disorder. I went to visit a few times with some of Kenneth's close friends. It seems there was no hope. We watched him continue to fail. It seemed an awfully long fight. One of his last requests was for his friends to bring him back some of his favourite foods. He knew it wasn't the best for him, but his friends wanted him to be happy. Kenneth didn't make it. He died a day or two later. I couldn't believe how heartless Jerry's profs were. They refused to either grant him an extension on his final projects, or arrange for alternate exam times. I wrote them pleading for compassion. To watch your brother, the only immediate family member die, and then need to help with funeral arrangements, cremation and all is bound to affect your ability to write exams, and continue to function. As Kenneth was born in the Year of the Dragon, every other Dragon attending the funeral was given a protective red ribbon as well as the usual coin and sweet candy. We went to the funeral and cremation where his closest friends burned twenty dollar bills as well as pretend money as in the Chinese tradition.

Life is definitely not fair.

A couple of Kenneth's friends went back to Taiwan. They are admirable fellows. They keep in touch.

As time flew by our student bases changed. We started with mainly students from Hong Kong. Gradually we got more Taiwanese and Koreans. By 1998 many came from Russia, Latin America, the Middle East and Africa.

CHAPTER TWENTY

GETTING TO KNOW BILL

Bill's challenging life bent and twisted him making him more pliable and understanding. His father died when he was three so he sought wisdom from his mother, his nurses and his foster mothers. Shortly after his father died leaving a pregnant wife and five other children his mom noticed him limping. She took him to the doctor: diagnosis; tuberculosis of the bone. He spent most of the next four years in the hospital getting his hip fused and his right femur repaired after breaking it accidently three times. He finished Grade Two in the hospital. Living in the hospital taught him to be patient, to be hopeful and to persevere.

At that point Children's Aid decided his mother couldn't get him healthy so they put him in foster care. His last foster mother was a widow in Chilliwack whose only son was in the merchant navy. She encouraged Bill in his schoolwork, treated him like a son and kept him looking forward to summer at Cultus Lake. When she became ill Bill was sent back home by Children's Aid.

At school some kids teased or taunted him. Usually Bill ignored them but sometimes there was a scuffle. Bill was a regular kid pushing boundaries, testing authority but never in serious trouble.

In his teen years he had two paper routes riding his bike and tossing the folded ones on to porches. He was reliable, on time and collected the money at the end of the month; the toughest part of the job. Later he set pins in a bowling alley and delivered groceries for the Red And White store. At the end of Grade ten he worked at a logging camp at Jordan River as a whistle punk. When a forest fire broke out the whole camp was conscripted to fight the fire. He went back to school that Fall but the call of the outdoors took him to work on a Bull Gang rigging spar trees in a camp on Sarita River at the end of Grade Eleven. That job used all the muscles you had. As the family needed money to pay for dental work his sister needed, he continued to work until Christmas. Then he went back to school.

Bill worked his way up in the forest industry from chaser to Government log scaler to log trader. He married, had three children. The boys played hockey and lacrosse. The girl took ballet and gymnastics. Bill delivered them to their activities, coached and helped manage the peewee lacrosse team. His life's challenges included dealing with mental health issues even his wife's suicide. In those days men kept their issues to themselves. He really didn't know where to turn .He got some counseling for himself and the kids.

After trying several housekeepers he decided to raise his family himself and did so until he remarried accepting two more children that are still part of his family. That marriage didn't last. Alcohol was the problem so he joined a men's Al-Anon group that supports families of alcoholics. Bill spent 15 years with them becoming a Round Up speaker in many places in BC. Life has taught Bill a lot. He is an easy going, patient, Italian perfectionist.

BILL, SHANNON, MARC

We both love the outdoors. He loved to fish, and hike. His job was inspecting logs anywhere in BC being purchased by Nichiman, a Japanese company. I had been a very active Girl Guide leader so we hiked, went to swap meets and got to know each other. By October we were holding hands. In November I got my first kiss. At Christmas we met each other's children. I met Bill's sons, Michael, and Marc, and his daughter, Shannon. He met my daughter, Nancy, and my homestays, Johnson, Hedy, Deborah, Ruby and Frank.

Just before Christmas I was approached to go to Asia to market the International Program. I was willing to go solo but I had four homestay students. I talked it over with Bill and was surprised when he proposed living in my house and taking care of the students when I was away. Wonderful!! This man was a great catch.

Hold on. There were a few glitches. After casually saying we would do something for my birthday he totally forgot. Then he suggested buying me chocolates as a peace offering and to go visit Nick as an evening out. Chocolates …no thought involved there…chocolates hmmm. And, going to see his friend Nick well that wasn't auspiscious either. Then, of course there was the time I was going to a movie with my cousin Pat and he said he'd probably come for tea after the movie so I didn't go out with Pat afterward. I came straight home. And waited. And waited.

We sat in the car and I explained my point of view. I am not okay with maybe. I had enough of that with my Dad. For me it is either yes or no; will or won't. None of this guessing game. Also, if you state a time or date that is it. My time is very valuable to me. I'll never forget the day I wanted to say Good bye to our friends in the morning and he assured me they would all be back for supper at 5 or 5:30 as he knew I had an appointment at 7pm. Well, they decided to play an extra round of golf but no one phoned me. I got there at 5—no one was home. I waited.

Then I heard my daughter's voice leaving a message. I didn't have a key. I needed to know what was up. I went to a pay phone and got Nancy's message. The meeting place had been changed. I went home made supper for Johnson and I. I took him to his driving lesson. I met Nancy. And I called Bill. I was furious. I told him I'd call him "Eventually" and hung up.

Yes, we learned to weed our garden. He was too used to living alone so no one else was affected if he changed plans but things were different now. Our relationship was stronger. We would each speak plainly, carefully explaining our perspectives and what we thought would work. Bill's time in Al Anon,an organization of support for relatives of alcoholics helped him understand we all have different needs and perspectives. He can always tell when there's a bur under my saddle-when we need to clear the air.

Life moved on we both kept busy. He was playing slow pitch ball, golfing regularly and working for Nichiman checking timber they wanted to purchase in Prince Rupert, Bella Coola or on the Fraser River. I was teaching school, caring for my homestays and sometimes renovating houses.

KELLY, KORI, RANDI, YVETTE IN THE UPPER PHOTO
BEN, HELEN, BILL, DELLA, ALBERTO.

One day in April 1993 he came up to me in the kitchen, gave me a hug from behind and said, "I want to be there for you for the rest of your life. I really want us to spend the rest of our lives together." My response was something like, "yes but we both need to be free to live our own lives as each of us sees fit and then our time together should be wonderful." " By that I mean that I will live life fully as I do now. I don't want you to solve my problems. That is my job. Don't try to stop me from overloading my plate. If I bite off more than I can chew I'll figure it out. You can't save me from myself. "I won't try to solve your problems either." In that case I'll be glad to live life with you forever. We have.

Twenty-six years later, we are enjoying our amazing love-filled journey together. Strangers often tell us what an inspiration we are. We radiate positive energy. We expect Six kisses when we leave home and six when we return. Sometimes I'm sure he can not count.

A Wedding!

You're married!

Well congratulations , so where ? When?

Oh, telepahic, I see. Well, why not, you sound very happy.

Having problems explaining it to his kids. They think your making a big deal out of something that visually never occured. You explained to them about the commitment ring last year.....And know you have a for sure ring. What's it like? Sounds beautiful.

You're taking him on a honeymoon. That should be nice. Will you see Sarah? Our family can't have a wedding without her it seems, which is nice.

Nice that there was some family at sis's elopement, even if she didn't plan there to be.

What a family. I don't think they planned the traditional wedding around us. Even if that's what that Japanese film crew thought they were getting when they came to film ours.

Mind you I don't know anyone else that has a 15 minute wedding movie clip , including commercails, and wildlife.

What does Sis think?

Getting use to her Mom is she?

Probably taking it better than if you married that fellow younger than her. Even if you had had a traditional wedding.

Sure the kids would be glad to call him Grandpa, we were getting pretty short on that commodity.

No, her boyfriend just goes by Harold. Doesn't want the families that closely combined I don't think. Maybe he feels it would create obligations.

So, are you going to live in one house now?

It seems to be working so far. Maybe if you ever move to Mission and built fresh. Thought any more on that?

Hey, what about receptions? Even when Sis eloped she ended up having Two.

No, I know she didn't think much of that. Figured she should have gotten marrid traditionally in the end as eloping didn't end all the formality and fuss anyways.

Telepathic reception?

Pat's having you over for a champange breakfast to celebrate, that's nice. Maybe telepahic receptions are like dinner

Chapter twenty-one persons of interest
Jeanette, Bill's homestay and her Mom from Qualicom beach   G o r d ,
her boyfriend
Yvette and her children

CHAPTER TWENTY-ONE

SHEEP'S PASTURES

My cousin, Sarah and her husband Don joined us for a golfing holiday. They got up at 3am and left Lake Chelan, Washington at 3:40 arriving in Oliver, British Columbia at 5:40am. After flying north from their home in Lake Forest, California, they rented a car that would carry their clubs and other necessities for the trip. We arrived from the coast at about 6:40am—after all –we had booked our tee time. We went to Fairview Mountain Golf Course for a shot gun start. [$106] We started on the seventh hole. None of us had played this course before so we were fascinated by the number of marmots on the course. The fairways were wide with lots of sand traps. I lost one ball and found two. I got 145-oh-oh; Sarah—I didn't get her score, Don got 91 and Bill 105. Maybe we weren't awake yet.

There were coyotes having a ten to twelve noon loud discussion on the third tee. It had looked like rain in the morning but it didn't materialize. When we left at 1:15pm it was hot. Sure glad our time was early. For lunch I had a delicious fruit salad. [$15]. We gassed up in Penticton [$17.25] and at Cache Creek [$9.90]. We had dinner at the Husky $17.25] and headed to the Sage Hills Motel for a bath and to bed. We were up at 6 am had breakfast at 7 and on the road by 7:45am after Viagra jokes, news articles and a US analysis of Canadian stocks.

At 8 am we learned that the First Nations had blocked off the road to Lillooet so we turned back to Lytton via Spence's Bridge. The air near Lytton smelled like a forest fire. We kept on towards Lillooet. Oops, a buck jumped in front of us. Bill wanted a photo so I stopped and Don just about ended up in the back seat. Finally we got to Lillooet and to Sheep's Pastures and to golf at around 11 o'clock by the time Sarah and Don had loaded up on every conceivable souvenir. Signs in the Ladies read Golf Forever....Housework whenever. They had a birdie tree-if you got a birdie you signed your name on a card and hung it on the tree.

Golf was challenging—long enough holes, rough fairways, sheep dung, irrigation systems and SHEEP, of course. We didn't need them to tell us when we made a BAAAD shot. I got 74 on nine holes. Bill got 46 [17 puts]. We took lots of pictures and had lots of laughs. We didn't hit any sheep either. They did make golfing a real challenge. We took photos of several scenic spots between Lillooet and Pemberton. I slept a good part of the way. We checked out Big Sky and their pro shop with Nike golf items on for half price. Don and Sarah bought towels for gifts. I noticed the Gordon Smith painting in the lobby area. We left for Whistler. Bill and I found the UBC Outdoors Club hostel on Nordic Way. We checked in. It was raining cats and dogs.

We met Sarah and Don for supper at Araxis'. It is well appointed, has excellent service and delicious food. I had Jonah's Crab Cakes with salad followed by a Hazelnut Meringue sandwich with fresh strawberries and whip cream filling on a plate drizzled with raspberry coulis and surrounded by four clumps of chocolate covered hazelnuts—out of this world. We were tempted to lick the plates!

Then off to visit with the fifty young adult French Canadians staying at the hostel. We loaded our stuff into space 42- one sleeping bag under and one on top. Then we went to the lounge area and soon became judges for a series of friendly contests between two groups. A very pleasant evening was had by all. To bed around eleven o'clock—to sleep—well we snatched a few hours but mostly we rested our bones not our brains even after the noisy chatter died down at three. By seven I was ready to get up and make breakfast- raisin, date, nut oatmeal, a banana and hot water to drink—just what the doctor ordered. The francophones dribbled into the kitchen, surveyed their unwashed dishes and individually made breakfast. Bill washed our dishes and we left for Pemberton Country Club amid a steady drizzle. But—

Surprise the sun was peeking through and we had a glorious day. Don shot 89, Bill 106, Sarah 118 and I got 120 [39 putts], very good for me. We started off at 10am and finished about 3pm—rather late for lunch but I had polished off a banana, two small boxes of raspberry cocktail and several handfuls of Olympic mix. Sarah and Don tied the putting contest. Lunch/Dinner was at the Santa Fe Café in Pemberton-I had a salmon unburger [no bun]; Bill and Sarah had Taco Salad and Don had cream of Broccoli soup and a veggie burger. We headed back to Whistler, stopped near Nairn Falls but it was too long a hike so we headed for Whistler Golf Course to check it out. We booked an 8:16 time for the next day. We decided to call it a day and each went our own separate ways only to meet again shortly after we bought ice cream cones at COWS. Don wanted a cone, Sarah stamps and postcards so I became the tour guide taking Sarah to the postcard shop, Don and I on to COWS then back to Bill and the Pharmasave for stamps. We parted again.

Bill and I bought groceries and headed for the hostel. We arrived, tried to sleep, but not the right time I guess, so we read, had a shower and off to sleep. I woke up at 4am –sneezing and itchy eyes, so I took half an antihistamine which put me back to sleep. Up shortly after seven feeling groggy—oatmeal and toast with peanut butter for breakfast. We were at the golf course by 8am and on the tee by 8:30am. The weather was a real mixed bag-a little sun, just enough to take your jacket off- then a cold or wet spell so you'd put it back on- sunglasses on and off, sunhat/rainhat on and off- at the end Sarah even put on her rain pants. The course is beautiful, playable and challenging. I lost two balls and found eight or so. Chipmunks scampered across a few times. There are two hanging baskets of flowers at each tee off spot. They are very attractive. I ate my banana and some more Olympic mix at about the nineth hole. Bill golfed really well and found lots of golf balls. He had a great day scoring 102 WOW. Don got 99, Sarah 120 and I got 139—must learn how to putt.

Lunch was late and I was grouchy. The food was expensive, service was slow and confused and the quality not near as good as Pemberton the day before. The waiter decided to hold our orders until Sarah came and she was busy getting Black Watch shorts, a green golf shirt and vest. They had to be tried on, compared, etc. It took too long for me and then when we asked the fellow for separate bills he bungled and didn't get both orders placed—Sarah's sandwich came turkey—she'd ordered egg salad and her second sandwich came before my chicken burger and Bill's smokie. I ate but it was bagged salad—not suitable for the type of establishment and ....you get the message..... After we finished Sarah and Don went shopping in the pro shop AGAIN.

Then we went to check out Nicholas North. There's a log cabin theme to the subdivision. The food looked better at Joel's [baking on display]. Next we checked out Chateau Whistler which is much like Banff Springs Hotel. Both courses looked attractive. This pro shop had some neat items but Whistler was still the best. There were fancy hand warmers made of Polar Fleece.

Back to the Village to the grocery store for more bananas and to Sarah and Don's room in Whistler Village Inn for wine [grapefruit juice for me], cheese [brie], crackers[Ry King for me], cherries [Rainier], Olympic mix and a good visit—time to just relax. Sarah and I stopped to check out Carlsbergs and she got Nicole a Haida design tapestry make up kit. She phoned cousin Jim to arrange their visit with Auntie Cathie. Bill phoned to get us a time at the Falls—9:06 am. We left Sarah and Don about 7:45 pm.

Back to the Hostel where the computer six were busy working on their program. A couple were making Chili—beef, peppers, onions---etc. The cooks knew what they were doing. There was a warm fire in the fireplace. Comfy. At 8:30 I made some cheddar cheese toast—our supper with glasses of grapefruit juice. I cleaned the microwave—my self designated hostel chore. Sarah and Don said the Village Inn provided a generous continental breakfast for guests, underground parking, comfortable bed, well-appointed rooms and the price was right. At that time Sarah had retired from teaching nursing at UCLA, Don was an orthopedic surgeon, Bill was still trading logs for Nichiman and I was teaching at NWSS. Every year we try to spend a week or two together, not always golfing. Sarah, my cousin, is like a big sister to me.

CHAPTER TWENTY-TWO

JEANETTE

Jeanette came to live with Bill when she began studying at SFU. Her Mom and family lived in Qualicum Beach on Vancouver Island so her Mom decided to find someone she could rely on to keep Jeanette safe so far from her home. Bill was like an Uncle. The family knew him well and his place was quite close to Simon Fraser University, a short bus ride away.

Bill set the rules for the house and Jeanette respected them. She was a very dedicated, tenacious student with the ability to plan for the future but she still had time to date. Fortunately Bill's habit of teasing [seriously] ; measuring each one of her dates for the coffin that he would provide if they harmed her in any way kept them laughing. When she met Gord it soon became apparent this relationship would last.

In the beginning Jeanette was focused on a degree in Criminology but my relationship with Jeanette and our many discussions about Canadian government policies and my involvement with the International students studying here led her to ask to observe my classes. The interactions in the class room led her to change her focus to be coming a dedicated educator, one who can influence youth to build a better society. She took a Certificate in Learning Assistance as well so she helps those with learning challenges.

Jeanette understands how difficult life can be if you have physical or mental handicaps but she, also, knows that each individual has to put a lot of personal effort into creating a good life. She helps her charges see what they can accomplish and facilitates their learning empowering and respecting each one. As an educator she keeps her standards high.

Jeanette and I keep in touch. She keeps me up-to-date on the changes in education in BC. When Gord and Jeanette decided to get married I was delighted when she asked me to be her matron of honour. Yvette and children arrived a few days before the wedding so they pitched in to help decorate the reception hall. The wedding was held in the Rose Garden on Burnaby Mountain. The sun shone, the bride and groom were perfectly attired, and we all helped them celebrate.

Gord and Jeanette now live in Chilliwack with their two young children. We visit when we can.

Chapter Twenty-two persons of interest

Homestays Frank and Ruby Bill, his friends, Charlie, Perry, Ross Rooney, Al Oloman, Tucker Brown, Rufus Moody, Noel and Margaret Smith.

My friends Ray and Sue Crossley and boys; Grace, my sister and her husband Shawn, Andrea, Jimmy and Kristy, Bill's nephew, Ben Jr. and his wife Donna and sons.

CHAPTER TWENTY-THREE

ON THE ROAD WITH BILL

"Let's pack the van and hit the road", said Bill. It was July 1994 school was out, so I was free. I left instructions with Frank and Ruby, on how to care for the house plants, and to water the lawn when necessary. Bill had packed his fishing tackle, and his chest waders. I'd taken books to read, and sketching materials. We both took our cameras.

We left early on Monday morning stopping at Hope for coffee at 9:30 am. It was a gorgeous day with just a few clouds skipping by. The Volkswagen Westfalia was a comfortable way to travel. We were at home anywhere. Our destination was Haida Gwaii.

Our first overnight was in the driveway of Ray and Susan Crossley in Prince George. It is always good to catch up with old friends. We hadn't seen the little boys yet. They were a happy bunch. They were contemplating a move to Courtenay or Comox.

In the morning we headed towards Prince Rupert to catch up with Bill's buddies from the many times he had been inspecting logs there for Nichiman. We saw Charlie and Perry of Sabre Marine, who made outstanding clam chowder for the gang every Friday. Later we met Ross Rooney of Rupert Printing who helped me produce the Final Edition of THE PLAIN TRUTH about Bill S. that I was having printed as a surprise for Bill on his 60th Birthday.

After catching up on the local news and visiting my sister Grace and family we took the ferry to Charlotte City. There we signed up for a zodiac tour of Ninstints. The zodiac took us near the shore then the husky fellow tossed us over his shoulder and deposited us on the beach. Wandering around under the huge Spruce trees we could see the mortuary poles, remnants of the native long houses, the rusting leftovers of logging equipment, even a lone moss covered caulked boot. The moss was everywhere, cushioning your feet, bringing its green gold beauty to the peaceful scene. Ninstints is one of those places where the reverence seeps into your spirit, your body, your bones. Being there is an experience you will never forget.

Checking out where Moresby camp had been; the Juskatla camp run by McMillan Bloedel and the Yakoun River were essentials for Bill.

However, he didn't want to go back to the spot that Crown Zellerbach had opened up when he was logging in the area. One day, his friend Al had borrowed a crummy [a crew carrying vehicle], so they eagerly explored the place, about a mile from tidewater. He was awestruck by the towering Sitka Spruce, the black-tailed deer feeding in the tall grass, and the crystal clear stream, where half a dozen steelhead trout, six to eight pounds each were relaxing unafraid. He felt this was the Garden of Eden, and he wanted to keep that memory intact.

En route to Masset, we saw the legendary Golden Spruce and several small deer. We golfed on the Air Force course in Masset, where I put ball after ball, off into the weeds. Bill kept advising me to slow down, take my time, but it was no use. Later, we went to the beach, where I found three beautiful moon snail shells. I was amazed by the number of huge crabs found in this area.

Returning, we stopped to see Tucker Brown, one of Bill's roommates years ago. We looked for Rufus Moody, the famous argillite carver, who had bunked with Bill, too, but he was away. Bill had logged on Haida Gwaii, for two years, as a young man. It holds a very special place in his heart. It is an incredibly, beautiful island chain. We left with memories that will last a life time.

Back in Prince Rupert, I picked up the printing from Ross Rooney. We touched base with Noel and Margaret Smith, then spent the night visiting the Loftus's. My sister, Grace, Andrea, Jimmy and Kristy were excellent company. Shawn was hung up at work so he came later. In the morning, we headed for the Copper River, so Bill could try his luck fishing. Bill has introduced me to many outstanding places in BC but the river didn't provide us with fish for dinner that night.

In Prince George we stopped for tea with Ray, Susan and the boys; then headed south. Kamloops was our last stop before home. We visited Ben Jr., his wife, Donna and their two sons. We rarely see them.

On this trip we took lots of photos, stored lots of memories but I didn't paint and Bill didn't catch any fish.

Home again. The houseplants didn't survive. When they remembered to water them, they left them sitting in water, so they drowned. No more tiny oranges.

We were all busy getting ready for school. I was, also, busy sending out invitations to Bill's surprise 60th Birthday Party at the end of September. I made 3- 9x13 carrot cakes that I put together to make one huge cake that I iced. I made or bought enough food for fifty people to come and go that afternoon. It was a great day. Bill was really surprised and he's kept his The PLAIN TRUTH about Bill S. safely stored all these years. We had what I call an Open House. The celebration went from 2pm to 8pm. We got some lovely photos of Bill's family and the small groups he belonged to.

THE
PLAIN
TRUTH

about Bill S.

THE VANCOUVER DAILY PROVINCE, FRIDAY, JU

"HOBO" BILL AND ADMIRERS—"Hobo" Bill and "Moke," his donkey, star perform
in the rodeo that comes to Vancouver next week, took time out from pre-rodeo cho
Thursday to visit the Crippled Children's Hospital, under auspices of city service clu
Above, three tiny inmates of the hospital get a great "kick" out of "Moke." Th
Freddy bursting with laughter as he pats "Moke," who's trying to pretend that he's use
all this attention. The other children are Billy and Mildred.

BILLY TO RESIGN AS
SEX SYMBOL   WHEN HE REACHES
GEORGE BURNS' AGE

BOGMAN BAFFLES
LOCAL EXPERTS
STRANGE HOLES   ATTRACT WORLDWIDE ATTENTION
SCIENTISTS GATHER TO
EXAMINE RARE FIND

Wee Willy Winky, who's really not so wee.

Wee Willy Winky ran through the forest, scouting logs here
and there. That one will make a bundle, and there's a good one
over there. Playing squirrel is a wonderful way to make a
living . If he could I'm sure he would, fly with the eagles,
swim with the trout, I wouldn't be surprised to find there's
some Haida in that Italian man's blood.

Wee Willy Winky hit the dance halls, saw a little lady in short ,
short, skirt. That sure put a twinkle in his eye. Now he asks
will it be my place or yours tonight? Married? with 2 houses.

Wee Willy Winky ran through the bases, in his baseball jersey.
Catch me if you can he grins, home plate is just ahead. A
child at heart forever, playing games. Mom says they haven't
found the "off" switch yet, I wonder what game that's in?
(Probably at the golf course.)

Wee Willy Winky ran around his pad "Has anybody seen my
putter ?" The rooster is crowing and it's time for golfing , I'll
break ninety yet, maybe before I'm sixty. He yells back," I'll
propably golf till.....till I decide to come home." Time is not an
issue, there is plenty ... either that or not enough to fit
everything in , so pack in as much as you can in case you
might miss something for lack of it, it's one of the two , I'm
sure. (P.S. Allen found a place in McGreggor that sells
Experienced golf balls, maybe that's what you need, or maybe
the ones you're using already have the wrong experiences ?)

Wee Willy Winky bought a new VW van, he packed it and gassed it, and put in his lady fine. Lets go a travelling, just you and me. I'll catch the fish and you can tell the tales. Tale #1, he forgot to pack...and.... But who needs those anyways when you've got your lady fine, and you're her King of Hearts?

Sixty!!! Finally found out your true age....Cradle robber ! Wild Bill (Hilcock) and his fateful hand, you may be just as wild at heart but I hope fate hands you a better hand.

Colourful like a wood duck that's the Bill I know,

Happy Birthday, young fellow.

(Remember you're only one up on Mom in height.)

Up the hills down the hills, shouting is everyone ready to celebrate ? Lets get at it .

Going down the logging road
with Ole Logger Bill,
Going down the logging road
up and over the hill-
Going down the logging road
looking for a speckled trou t.
Going down the logging road-
are you su re you know
the way back out?

Lucky Billy

I wonder of Bill will remember the first time we ever went skiing?

We were about 13 years old when an acquaintance of his named Dave who lived on Windsor Street, offered to take us skiing. He was older than us—going to Vancouver Tech.--and planned to take us to the Vancouver Tech cabin situated halfway between Westlake and the old Hollyburn Lodge.

Kenny Willan, Bill and myself, led by Dave, left for Westlake Lodge on a cloudy Sunday morning. Unlike today, there were no chairlifts and the only way to the Lodge was to travel by bus to what was then the top of the British Properties and then to hike in an upwards direction for the next 2 1/2 hours. As I'm sure he remembers, our city legs were not used to this type of effort and we arrived at Westlake Lodge tired and hungry.

At the Lodge we rented our skiis which in those days consisted of solid hickory skiis with cable bindings and leather boots. Once we had assembled our equipment and were ready to go, Dave took the lead going as what appeared to us neophites as a bat out of Hell! Struggling through the snow (and by now it was snowing) we finally arrived at the cabin and were desperately looking forward to a hot lunch—but after an hour of unsuccessfully trying to light the stove with damp wood which did nothing more than to smoke us out of the cabin, we reluctantly donned our gear once more and began our long journey back towards the Lodge and their cafeteria.

Up to this point in time, our 'skiing' had been all uphill, but now—for the first time—we were to ski DOWNHILL with no instruction whatsoever on how to accomplish this feat. It waseveryman for himself and we tried to keep up with Dave to the best of our combined abilities. Needless to say, we soon fell behind and contented ourselves with following his ski-tracks through the fresh snow- which worked well until we came to a 'Y' in the trail. Not knowing which set of tracks belonged to Dave, we took a chance, Instead of arriving at the bottom of the hill by the Lodge we ended up at the top of a horrendously steep hill known as "The Graveyard" ski run, one of the steepest hills on the mountain... if a person stood at the top of this hill (as we were) and looked straight down, you could see the front door of the Lodge.

Ken Willan was the first to attempt the slope, stumbling, floundering and falling every few feet. I was next and did the same. Bill, who waited until we began our descent and thinking he was much cleverer than us, began to side-step down until he got to the half way point. Once ther, he pointed his skiis downhill and schussed straight downward toward the front door of the Lodge, thinking he would come to a stop at the bottom of the hill where we were standing. HE WAS WRONG!

Bill whizzed by us at about 30 mph, straight for the front door. Our yelled instrustions for him to fall were ignored--no doubt because of his stark fear—as he continued towards the door FULL SPEED AHEAD. Fortunately for him, within eight feet of the door was a small bump which sent him flying ass-over-teakettle into a snowbank alongside the door, rather than into it.

This is how Bill was Baptised 'Lucky Billy" on future ski trips.

BILL AND HELEN 1948

HEIGH HO, HEIGH HO, IT'S OFF TO WORK WE GO...

IN CAMP WITH A POWERSAW--LOGGER BILL

Perry of Sabre Marine in Prince Rupert, told me of the time when Bill had gone out in a boat to check some logs. Five o'clock came, no Bill--six came and went-- still no Bill--at seven they decided they had better go and check--at seven thirty they found Bill on a boom and the boat in the middle of the harbor! Bet he was glad to see them.

MR. MOM....

In today's world of single parents I have decided to tell a story of a clan named the SPAGNUT'S. The clan comprised of -father Bill,[dalias moneybags]; Mike [the old one]; Marc [the middle one]; and Shannon { the baby one}. Indeed it may be said that going it solo with kids in tow is no easy task.

The housekeepers changed as often as a politician changes his or her tone. They came in all shapes and sizes. There was his sister, Mary who even with her tough methods had little success controlling the bunch. It then became time to change the guard. In came his neice, Lori who, overwhelmed by the task was out of the picture very quickly. Then there was the old bozer who drank and even walked away with some of his stuff. In came a young lass whowas very nice and for a while the house ran like a clock. However in six months time she was on her way. After Cindy came Lenora, a beautiful young women who he had a hard time turning down especially since summertime meant sun tanning in the yard--in a bikini, of course. Even though she was a hot one [so I hear] he had to let her go because the housework didn't do itself. So,- left with a sour taste for housekeepers Bill decided to shoulder a dual role for his kids. All was not going smoothly in the household and to try to control the home, Mike asserted himself and became a pseudo-parent.At times it seemed to Dad at work that every five minutes one of the kids would phone to complain about another. The kids were reaching a stage when they were wrapped up in their own lives. During tense moments he would say "I just want harmony" It was clear to him that not having their mother at home left an emptiness which would be hard to fill. Therefore we salute those single parents out there who barely manage to hold it together--especially ones like Bill Spagnut who ddeserves a gold star for his effort. GOOD JOB! BILL.

Marc, Shannon, Bill, and Mike   no wonder he went hunting!!!!!

QUEST FOR STEELHEAD
KIDS IN TOW...

Bill had always aroused interest in his children with tales of the
MIGHTY THOMPSON STEELHEAD--ooh, they were kings in the fishing
sport.

wishful and hopes high the Spagnut clan embarked on their trip to
the infamous Thompson River. Kept occupied by the beautiful valley
and mountains and the usual bickering between them the siblings
managed to contain their anticipation. THE BIG ONE WAS AT HAND AS
THEY REACHED THE HOT SPOT.

They geared up and headed down to the meat hole as it was called
because it used to produce so many fish. deeply concentrated
efort, skill and working the hole like a bunch of professionals
resulted in the loss of gear and bait only.--Their heads down they
trudged back to the camp for dinner and conversation. After
reviving their spirits with spirits and more fish talk they went
to sleep early vowing early in the morning to land the king.
Morning came and they were out at the hole at daybreak. They
worked the hole using every lure, bait,and item of gear they had
without success. Two of the sons left to go motorbiking in the
hills no longer spirited fishermen. The rest remained persistently
pursueing the elusive steelhead. Marc and Ron returned to camp at
dinner to hear that Dad had ' a good bite!' OO1 AHH!"
On their return voyage the kids were the stress levels arguing and
complaining about fishing. Dad drove his usual *mach five* yet
avoided the smokies. Things quieted down and Dad once again, the
nostalgic father drifted off into his glory days --memories--But
the troops didn't bite this time --NO--they just wouldn't bite,
unlike the big one that got away.

Al Oloman

Bill Spagnut

George Tickell

SPORT'S PAGE

Bill has always been a sports enthusiast. He started off with both baseball and fishing at an early age. I as never able to ascertain if these activities were designed to keep him away from chores or if they were passions but since he still pursues both I'll opt for the latter. I have learned that Bill swam, skated and played badminton as well. However, it seems that one of his favorite sports was chesterfield rugby--remember Beatrice F.?

Bill encouraged his children to get involved with sports, too. He was a supportive parent who coached lacrosse and watched hockey. Between work, being a househusband and trying [and succeeding] to coach teams and ferry kids his life must have been hectic indeed.

BEST WISHES
THE KINGFISHERS
TOM PROTHEROE
BOB HAZLETT
GEORGE TICKELL
AL OLOMAN
BRIAN STELMACK
BRUCCE GERHART
PHYLLIS MALM

The International Brotherhood of
Golfers Anonymous

- We would like to wish
Bill S. a Happy 60th

Birthday!

We also would like to
proclaim him as the
*"Hacker with
Yellow Balls!*

CONGRATULATIONS from
Nick, Arnie, Terry, Jim,
Don and Dennis

REGRETS FROM
DOUG KLEINSORGE in the Portland Marathon
Jim Russell in a Golf Tournament
Perry, Ross, Tom, Bob and the Loftus Family too far away to attend

Congratulations from the VILLAGE INN DIEHARDS

Don
Barb
Gary
Shawn
Sharon
Randy
Cindy
Ken
Carl

Darcy
Laine
Ray
Barbs
and the rest
of the team.

Bill has always been ready to sacrifices his body for the game --skinned legs, bent fingers and even stopped the ball with his head--OWW!

BEST WISHES FROM CHARLIE AND THE CHOWDER GANG

Horace, Alan, Norman, Randy, Ted and the others at Sabre Marine

PHOTO OF
BILL
CHARLIE
AND
PERRY

Anticipating another 60 years for the special guy of my special friend.
Ellen

Chapter twenty-three persons of interest
Bill and I; Terry and Mary Colin [Shannon's in laws]; Yvette and family
The Parthenay Clan—in Manitoba and Washington State

CHAPTER TWENTY-FOUR

PARTHENAY REUNION

The Invitation to the Parthenay Reunion arrived early in the Spring of 1996. We planned our times carefully, packed our tent and looked forward to meeting so many members of the family at one time.

En route,Bill and I stayed in the Hostel in Banff after a long day driving. We were lucky to get a couples room. We enjoyed the camaraderie there. We heated a can of Chili for supper and turned in for the night. Breakfast was easy, granola and yogurt. Soon we were on our way down to the prairies. Just out of Medicine Hat we spotted the antelopes bounding southward; such elegant creatures.

We arrived at Terry and Mary's in Regina in the afternoon. They organized a game of golf for the next morning and we decided to visit the RCMP Museum in the afternoon. We had a great time but almost had to pry Bill out of the museum. The next morning we were on our way to Portage la Prairie to Yvette and Allen's farm thankful for the kindness of our generous hosts in Regina.

The Saskatoon berry harvest was just over but there were a lot of bits and pieces to finish up. Randi, Kori and Kelly were happy to see us. Yvette took us to Delta Marsh. We all put on life jackets and went canoeing in an area maintained by Ducks Unlimited. On our way back we stopped at Duke's place for Yvette to sort out a project they were working on.

The Reunion was the 2nd, 3rd and 4th of August so we all went north to Ste. Rose du Lac. Soon there was a tent city on Denis and Donna's lawn.

The local Parthenays hosted relatives from Vancouver, Washington; Red Lake Road, Ontario and other places I cannot remember.

What was my/our connection to the Parthenay Family? Alexis and Leonie Parthenay were the parents of Leon who never married, Jeanne who married Alfred Etienne Dheilly and had George[my husband], Gilles never married and Odile who married Alfred Chardon. Next in line was the Marcel and Marie-Rose Parthenay's family of Denis, who married Donna; Donald who married Valerie and their children Aaron and Lisa; next was Gilles and Heather and last in that family, Joanne who married Donald Saquet. This family hosted the reunion. The baby of the original pair was Jules. He married Berthe and they produced Annette, Rita, Raymond, Daniel, Paul, Jeanine and Louise.

LUELLA AND JACK PARTHENAY showing his track and field award.

Following our marriage June 11th, 1960 George and I went on several honeymoons. The first was to visit Charlie and Mary Kaake in Vancouver, Washington. Mary Kaake was born Marie Parthenay so she was George's Great Aunt. Her only son Georges Guillot was killed in the war. Since she had no other children she passed some of her family treasures on to me and to Yvette when Yvette was born.

While we were in Vancouver, Washington George took me to visit his Great Uncle Eugene and Aunt Tillie. Eugene was a great collector of old toys. He had a monkey that climbed a stick and a can that when you turned it it said "moo" and many other old fashioned, collector's items. Eugene and Tillie had two children, Jack and a daughter who lived in Richland.

My other favorite of George's Great Aunts was Genevieve. She was the youngest of the Vancouver, Washington Parthenays. She and her husband Ron farmed, fished, hunted, clammed –you name it they did it. They explored the mountains and streams. We became a mutual adoration society. Visiting her for breakfast you got green eggs [duck eggs] and ham. For lunch the world's best clam chowder. At that stage of my life I was making jams and jellies, vying for the best breads, cakes and cookies at local fairs and the Pacific National Exhibition. We both grew large gardens, too. We went to all of their funerals George, his Mom and I . Before that the letters flew back and forth.

Some of Jack and Luella's kids are the same ages as our Yvette, Nancy and Marcia were so we visited them once or twice a year. They were great company, loads of fun—we wished they lived closer.

The same year I met the Washington Parthenay's George took me to Manitoba to meet the Dheilly's and Parthenay's there. In St. Boniface we met Annette Parthenay and her family. Then the Bourdon's, the Morrier's, and the Raymond Dheillys' . We kept going to Laurier to meet Grandpa Etienne Dheilly and his wife, Euphemie. George's Uncle Emile and Marie lived in a tiny, tiny house. I have no idea how they fit all of their seven plus children in.

Visiting the Ste. Rose du Lac Parthenay's George stopped at Marcel and MarieRose's place first. There we got directions to Leon's farm where Grandma Leonie lived. Everyone said "You won't be able to understand her but Leon will explain". Well, it was just the opposite. Her French was sharp, clear and quickly spoken. Leon's soft, slow not so easy to follow. Back in BC they had told me Berthe and Jules would be the best hosts but we have always had a kinship with Marcel's bunch. Funny isn't it. They are all good company but some you feel more at home with. I'll never forget Grandmere running down the steps apron floating, hollering, "George, George, mon petite cher George.! She insisted we take back the photo—professionally taken of George's Mother when she was three. Such a treasure. George's Mom was definite she didn't want it. We happily hung it over Yvette's bed. The next year we had Yvette and the following Nancy was born and two Parthenay family's had a little Joanne named after me. I hadn't met Rita Le Conte's Joanne until the Reunion and by then I had totally changed my name. Many of the people I mentioned died before the Reunion but our relationships are still strong. We see each other as often as we can and we write letters every Christmas. Like Aunty Cathy, Marcel, MarieRose and Denis are the sort of people who draw people to them. They are like magnets. Life revolves around them.

Chapter twenty-four persons of interest
Yvette, Randi, Kori, and Kelly Ruby, her father and Mother
Vincent, his parents Loise Chen, a former student
My brother Ross, his wife, Pat, son Nate and daughter Kushanda
Masahiro,,his Boss, his friend Goichi Motoko
The Iyama family-Kuniko, Yukio, Mikko, Momo. Kazuaki Kanako

CHAPTER TWENTY-FIVE

1998

When Yvette, my eldest daughter was left a few dollars by her grandfather in his will she decided to take herself and her three children Randi eleven, Kori nine and Kelly seven, to explore Asia. I agreed to go with them. I couldn't pass up a chance to get to know my grandchildren better and be part of the adventure. We planned to visit Ruby and her parents, the Liao's, in Taipei as Ruby had lived with me for a few years. Vincent Sung had stayed in my home, too. Louise Chen was a former student. From Taipei we went to Kuala Lumpur, on to Bali, next to Lombok to visit my brother Ross, his wife, Pat and son Nate. Then we would go back through Japan staying with Masahiro Yamaguchi, who had been one of my many homestays and seeing most of my friends there. It would take about six weeks.

We packed carefully as each of us had to be able to manage our own luggage---even the littlest had his own backpack. We had to be as frugal as possible without being stingy. The first leg of our journey took twenty hours and we lost a day crossing the international dateline.

We arrived at the Chiang Kai-Shek International airport around midnight expecting to be met by Ruby's dad. After we claimed our luggage we looked everywhere but he just wasn't there. As neither Yvette nor I spoke Chinese we were at an extreme disadvantage. I had Liao's address and Frank Chien, another homestay's phone number but I called several times and no one answered. After 2am the airport was almost empty. Finally a kind taxi driver came over and said he would take us to the Liao's home. Even he had to go around the area twice before he found the right place. By then it was between three or four in the morning. We rang the doorbell. When they came down they said "You are supposed to come tomorrow! We are so sorry".

We settled in. Cotton sheets on hardwood floors –not the most comfortable, with pillows for our heads we slept till the streets came alive. Ruby's mom, Liao tai-tai made a special breakfast for us, rice soup [congee] that you could add pickles, peanuts or other items to. It was totally unfamiliar so the boys were reluctant to try this new cuisine. Mrs. Liao, who ran a small café, tried everything she could think of to get the boys to eat. It was a challenge but the yellow watermelon was fine.

The first day we drove around in a van with Ruby's parents. We all laughed when a Taiwanese boy about five or six years old riding on a scooter behind his Mom pulled his eyes wide open--- exactly the opposite to what we used to do here when I was a child. We saw the koi swimming in the pool outside the Sun Yat Sen National Monument, the ferns as big as trees in Yangmingshan Park and the fumaroles spouting sulphurated steam on the mountain side. But the strongest memory is of the hordes of scooters and motorbikes zooming around Taipei. They made a steady buzz.

We went to the night market. The kids tried catching goldfish. At the Snake market we were told if you drink their blood you will become courageous. Would you? We watched Tae Kwon Do learning to always keep your hips square and to pay attention to both halves of your body. We visited a three hundred year old temple, Lung-Shan with intricate carvings where you could pray for help with your exams and many other things.

Another day we went to the zoo by the Metro. We looked at all the animals and the special exhibits. There were no pandas but they were working on an Arctic exhibit. I hope it would be refrigerated as we'd been perspiring since we got off the plane. About 11 am I started asking where I [later called "The Dragon"] could buy some snacks but Vincent's parents had told him to not let me pay for anything. My repeated requests were ignored. They didn't know I get violent headaches if I don't eat regularly. We finally left the zoo at about 1pm. We took the Metro into the city. By then it was pouring rain--- warm but drenching.

We tried to take a taxi to the restaurant but we needed two taxis so we split up. Yvette and Randi went with Louise Chen in one. Kori, Kelly, Vincent and I rode in the other. There was a misunderstanding between Vincent and Louise so the taxis ended up at different restaurants in different parts of the city. I was very stressed. My head was pounding. I think Vincent had been in Canada too long and Taipei had changed. While we waited for Vincent to sort things out with his Mom and Louise I had got Vincent to buy the boys a drink. Yvette and Randi were okay as Louise took care of them. I think she was studying tourism at the time.

Anyway we didn't get together for lunch until 3:30. It was a Mexican restaurant. I was totally stressed out and unreasonable. I kept ordering tortillas and they kept sending chips. On top of that I was worried about the cost and since we were late and starving we ordered a lot of food. I know I was sharp. I embarrassed Yvette. I felt a lot of responsibility for what had happened yet I felt helpless to change things. Louise and Vincent were afraid their parents would chew them out over the mix up, too.

As it was hot and humid after we got back to Liao's we headed to a grocery store to buy ice cream to cool off. They had chocolate ice cream but Ruby suggested corn ice cream something we don't have here. Everyone got a corn ice cream cone but no one really liked them so they gave them all to me and I ate as much as I could to be polite. I was covered in melted ice cream. Everyone was still hot.

Have you seen an Asian toilet? Our first time was at the Chinese Movie Museum where the kids watched "Mulan." Later that evening we took our hosts for dinner. Kori tried chicken's feet and liked them. He didn't know what they were. At Chiang Kai- Shek's monument the boys tried to make the water filled brass bowl sing. We watched a man mouth paint and turn out lovely work. Our last memory of Taipei is of an open air flower market several blocks long under a highway overpass.

Soon we were on the plane heading to Kuala Lumpur, what an airport, so modern and spacious. At the hostel Kelly and I shared a small room as we both snore. The others had a slightly larger room. We were staying in a youth/backpacker's hostel on the edge of the Chinese market. The next day I stayed behind to get over my headache.

Yvette and the kids went to the Orchid Garden, and the Butterfly House that had huge, dramatic ones and many unusual species. Spectacular. There were monkeys- wild along the roadsides. Entertainment was everywhere. Later we checked out many intricate batiks and local carvings. We went to the Batu caves climbing 272 steps to the first entrance. There were pigeons and monkeys wherever you turned. You had to make sure you hung on to your belongings. When we came back to the hostel to rest or discuss plans the boys were kept entertained watching the rats climb the staircase.

After having watermelon for breakfast we went to the National Mosque and Prayer Hall. Then on to the Bird Aviary which was as perfect and as colourful as the Butterfly House. So many things to see. At that time Kuala Lumpur had the highest twin towers in the world and the third highest building. We were all fascinated by one parking system that put the cars on a conveyor belt and deposited them up on different floors for whatever length of time necessary. Haven't seen that in our area yet.

The airplanes had video terminals at each seat so the kids were happily occupied. We could look down and admire Indonesia's beautiful coastlines. When we landed in Denpasar the capital of Bali we had to keep our eyes on our own luggage as there were busboys everywhere. We didn't have any local currency so a fellow took Yvette to get her money changed. She changed fifty American dollars and came back with a fist full of bills. The fellow who had helped her took his fee and helped us get a taxi to Ubud. Yvette realized he took as much for his tip as the driver charged us for driving us all the way to Ubud, an Indonesian Arts and Crafts center.

Ubud, a verdant paradise, was about two hours inland. We had decided to look for accommodation on Monkey Forest Road. The driver took us to Warsi's cabins, a great place. It backed onto a rice field. We could watch the farm workers and the beautiful white birds come and go. Peaceful. We had a spacious room with two double beds and a cot. We had our own bathroom and water for the shower was solar heated. Breakfast was an egg and banana hotcakes. Tea was available anytime. They even offered free babysitting! All this for the five of us for sixteen Canadian dollars per night.

The boys got to play soccer with the locals. We checked out a few of the local eateries often having Nasi Goreng and Chicken Satay. One Day we had Chicken GORDON Blue. On Independence Day we got to watch the young fellows shiny up greasy poles in a competition for treasures. Yvette and Randi took a batik lesson while the boys and I trekked around the area on a route laid out by Yvette. We really explored Ubud thoroughly. We walked past all of the fields each with daily offerings usually on woven banana leaf holders of rice, and fresh flowers. Everyone took time to light incense and say a prayer at the start of the day. Be careful where you walk as they are all over the sidewalks in town. "Deal for you." "Morning Price." "Good for you, good for me." A shopper's paradise. Yvette bought a dress for two dollars Canadian. We considered musical instruments, batiks, ikat weavings, even silver jewelry.

We took another long walk in the country and saw people carrying bamboo bundles on their heads, people bathing in ditches and more. We didn't get lost and arrived at the Pura Pentaran Sasih Temple with the 2000 year old bronze drum. Huge. Legend says it fell from the sky and is the "Moon of Pejeng". Women's legs must be covered to enter these temples so sarongs are available to rent. In open kitchens fueled by coconut husks we saw them preparing rice in coconut milk and woven offerings. Now they use large wooden cylinder drums to call the residents to the temple.

Further along we found the Elephant Cave, a shrine to Ganesh, a Hindu God. There were bas-relief carvings and ceremonial holy baths for good luck, too. Then we decided to take a local bus home. For fifty cents for the five of us-- it was well worth it.

Independence Day is August seventeenth, a formal celebration with drill teams from the schools, everyone in uniform, bands and a sports day with prizes. The government only sponsors school up to Grade Four. Most children do not continue after they turn twelve.

For me the highlight of our time in Ubud was the funeral ceremony for a prominent local fellow. Apparently they bury their dead for a few years until they can afford to have an impressive parade followed by cremation. The parade had tiered pagoda-like shrines carried on about fifty young men's shoulders. These shrines carried the bodies of the prominent fellow, another adult and a child. Beautiful young girls in sedan chairs carried by more young men followed and in turn they were followed by gift bearers bringing live birds, money, food, clothing or fancy cloth all to be cremated with the body. The crowds brought water bottles to keep the men hydrated. It was a long procession ending in a field of uncut grass where the huge black papier- mache bull sat waiting for the bodies to be inserted so it could be set on fire.

When we got to the field Yvette found some snakeskins so we became worried about snakes. What if they were poisonous! On the way back she stopped at a stand that sold water, snacks and fruit but when she asked if what she had was snake skin the store lady was puzzled but nodded, 'Yes it is". Then one of us a few days later spotted the fruit that had a skin like a snake—we inquired. It was called Snake Fruit and tasted like pineapple.

The ceremony seemed to have taken forever and the taxi driver we had hired to bring us out wanted to get back to Ubud. We left.

For a change of pace after Ubud we went to stay at the beach at Candidasa for a few days. The bungalow had a lagoon on one side and a garden on the other. It faced the clear, blue ocean. A perfect place to relax. While there Kelly helped a local family gather seaweed. Kori found something of interest on the beach and came running back to tell me but stopped totally shocked when he opened the cabin door and saw me naked on the bed getting a massage. He turned and ran and ran. When asked what spooked him he said, "You don't want to know".

Here the people were very poor, bathing in ditches, wanting to do anything for you; to braid your hair, take you out fishing, go snorkeling, or massage you. The porters continued to try to take our packs when we went to get on the ferry. It wasn't a fancy ferry. We were on it for six hours crossing to Lombok.

My brother Ross, his wife Pat and son Nate lived there. Getting off the ferry on Lombok was a nerve rattling experience as once the gangplank was down a swarm of young people wanted to take everyone's luggage. It was a job to keep us together and for each of us to carry our own gear.

KELLY AND HIS LOAD

We stayed at a place a couple of blocks from Ross's complete with small lizards and more cold showers. Ross and Pat made sure we saw the highlights. At some place we traveled Kelly saw the people doing their laundry and bathing in the lagoons and rivers. It puzzled him so he asked "Why don't they do that at home?" Yvette had to tell him lots of those people didn't have water at home.

We went with Pat to the Muslim Pearl Market. Prices were good. We bought a few keepsakes. Did you know pearls come in blue, black, yellow, copper, pink and even lime green. Pat knew where the best bargains were and what to watch for. We went to the open market with meat, flies and stinky fish that Pat's driver couldn't stand. Please not the FISH market.

Ross got home from Sumbawa where he was working opening a copper mine.

That island was originally inhabited by head-hunters and poisonous snakes and some of them are still there. Ross rented a boat to take us to the Gili Islands but he was conned. No boat, no driver. No problem he found another. Part of that deal was for us to get a ride in a chidomo or donkey pulled cart. That is a favored kind of transportation on Lombok. Then we got into a glass bottom boat to see the corals, the tropical fish, turtles and all. Too bad the gas fumes were so bad. We stopped at three islands, saw some blue coral and Yvette and Randi swam with one large turtle. I'm sure for Yvette, Randi and the boys snorkelling and swimming with the sea turtles at Gili Tarawanga will be an unforgettable experience.

About this time Randi got a strep throat so Pat took her to the doctor.

We were treated to lunch at a classy South seas-type resort at Kuta beach which looks like a Hollywood confection. There I looked at the prices [$233,500 rp!] and told everyone we should just have water. The prices seemed astronomical till Yvette figured out the exchange rate. The prices were roughly equivalent to those at home. [only $30 Canadian for our lunch] . The architecture, the mosaics walkways, the swinging reclining chair with the alligator carved armrests and a person fanning you with a banana leaf what more could you want?

We were able to visit an indigenous village; see how they lived and to purchase their weaving. While there one of the women gave Randi her baby to hold. She told her " next time bring diapers." It seems to me we packed a lot into the time we were on Lombok. We saw a wedding parade. I heard that marriages are arranged when kids are about ten and the male has to pay a dowry of chickens, goats even water buffalos to the bride's family when they marry at eighteen. Houses here have two rooms one for the males and one for the females. They only get together when they want to have children. The cooking is done outside. The roofs are thatched and the floors are made of mud and cow dung. We visited another village where we bought magic teapots and whistles shaped like animals.

Yvette, Randi and I ran in something called a Hash House Harriers run following a trail of shredded paper.. That was up and down behind farms, passed the pigs and children looking for gifts of money or sweets and, and…. I'm not sure how I survived that as I'm not athletic at all. In the end Yvette had to come back for me. We got in more shopping---batiks, kites, sarongs,. Kelly bought a conch shell and learned how to blow in it and have all the land hear him.

We look back and laugh when we think of Ross's driver who thought he was something special because his wife had a baby three months after they married. He was a miracle man.

KORI. A NEW FRIEND, KELLY

A NEW FRIEND AND RANDI

Time to pack and find our way back to Denpasar. Andy, Ross and Pat's driver, arranged for a charter bus and luxury ferry. No porters---so much better than our trip in.

On our way back to Denpasar a fellow on the bus couldn't believe we were there during the political unrest. He set us up with a taxi and a place to stay. The owners of the inn had a girl Randi's age. They were having a good time together so when it neared time to go to the temple they asked if Randi could go with them. Yvette and Randi thought that would be fine so they dressed Randi in one of the daughter's outfits and Randi went. At some point they put rice on everyone's forehead. Randi wondered why the rice stayed on everyone's forehead but hers fell off. The daughter and Randi were pen pals for a few years and they met again about eleven years later. Before we left we traded our local papers for some in English. Yvette had had Montezuma's Revenge on Lombok and she wasn't perfectly healthy but much better.

From Denpasar we went back to Kuala Lumpur overnight courtesy of the airline and caught another high tech plane to Narita airport outside Tokyo. Before we got off the plane Yvette explained she had a list of wanted to see places in Japan and things she wanted to do. She didn't want to get stuck with visiting my friends everyday. I asked for a list and we pretty well met her requests. Getting off the plane in Narita Yvette was checked for cholera. Luckily she didn't have it.

ROXSANE with Kelly, MASA
with KORI AND RANDI in front in Portage 1990ish.

We were met by Masa who had stayed with me for a couple of years. We took the train back to a station where several of my friends were waiting for us. We had a short visit at MacDonald's and then headed to Masa's apartment where he had futons for all of us and we could cook in his kitchen. I believe he had recently broken up with the young woman he had hoped to marry. There were boxes and boxes which we offered to unpack but he said his wife would do it.

Masa was an excellent tour guide, too. Japan was different. We rode the subway, saw monks praying waiting for money, students in uniforms, lots of bicycles. Yvette wanted to see Chinatown in Yokohama. We went for dimsum which we all enjoy so that was special. We saw the fancy temple with the curved roof and intricately carved pillars but I liked the stone dogs and lions that protect the site.

RANDI, KELLY AND KORI AT GOTOKUJI TEMPLE

Yvette wanted to go to a temple so we went to Gotokuji to the famous cat temple where legend has it that a sleeping cat kept the samurai hidden from those searching for him. Because of this the cat is seen to bring good fortune. You see these cats with their paws up in many businesses all over the world. There was a gong to ring so you get the attention of the god who will answer your prayers. We bought fortune papers. Randi got the best one and Yvette the least so following Japanese tradition she tied her paper to a tree to see if the wind would change her fortune. For me we went shopping for washii paper for my Art.

We went to a Sushi bar for supper. It had a revolving belt of food to choose from. Yvette told the kids they had to eat whatever they chose. Kelly chose three desserts. The rest of us tried a few different things.

Yvette wanted to see how their schools worked so Mitsue [Mikko] Iyama organized a visit to her daughter's class. Randi taught them to play Head's Up Seven Up. Randi, Kori and Kelly were surprised to see vegetable gardens at school as well as chickens, rabbits, peacocks, ducks and carp. The students have access to them at all times to care for them and make observations. In Japan you are tested to see if you are smart enough to go to a public school like this one. If not you go to a private school. School is on every second Saturday as well. As a school trustee in Portage Yvette really appreciated Mikko's help.

Masa took us to a park where old buildings have been preserved for their heritage, temples, pagodas, noblemen's homes, other homes all beautifully kept.

One weekend Iyama's family organized a huge birthday for Motoko and Kuniko that was really a welcome party for us as all my old friends were invited. We made a chocolate Marshmallow rice krispie cake for them. This party was in the Kanamorimae community center. Kazu, Kanako, and Momo the Iyama grandchildren kept us all entertained with a watermelon bashing contest. There was lots of traditional food, and presents for all. The kids got to light one firecracker each. Masa brought very well chosen gifts for the children. That and staying overnight in the senior's center where Motoko lives were probably the highlights of our stay in Japan.

When I first heard we were invited to stay with Motoko I thought there was no way this can work. The center where she lives is like a 'Hilton' for wealthy seniors. It has classy artwork, sculptures, fountains and a care center in case you are not well. So, I told everyone not to bring their pyjamas. We would have to go back to Masa's. Well, it didn't work out that way. Motoko had futons and pyjamas for all of us. We had lunch together. At the entrance to the dining room there are three featured meals to choose from. You just have to ask for A, B, or C. We all ate together then Masa went home. As Motoko's friends we were important so everyone was bowing and greeting us warmly.

We went to Motoko's English class. The teacher knew the kids were coming so she brought games for them to play. Then we went outside for exercise and to learn how to spin tops. Randi got a minor scrape.

Now it was time to have a bath in the ladies communal bath! There was no way out of it. Kelly was not going to have a bath. He had had one the day before. So I said okay he has to do homework while we have a bath. Kori went first he had a shower, dressed and climbed into the massage chair. Randi was next. She had a shower. Yvette was next. She didn't want to try the Japanese Onsen system either. She had a shower, too. I don't think you can imagine the place.

There were rows of shelves with baskets on them. You put your clothes in the basket and moved from place to place naked. Everyone did and there were quite a few ladies seventy, eighty, even ninety years old there. I was last but I knew the system. Clothes off. Go to the room set up so several women could have their own station with a plastic stool and a set of taps to wash their hair, use a telephone type shower to get clean and rinse all the soap off before getting in the big Jacuzzi style tub with all the other ladies. Relax. Get out, get dry, get dressed and collect the crew to go for supper.

Supper was in a reserved room---we got the full royal treatment. Then Motoko taught us origami and how to write a little Japanese. Yes, we stayed over night, had a delightful breakfast and left with Masa before lunch with two wedding kimonos worth at least ten thousand dollars each to take home. We went to Sizzlers for lunch where we met Masa's boss. Her daughter gave Randi a penguin backpack.. Randi had picked up or come down with a bladder infection so Masa's boss took her to the doctor. Goichi, Masa's buddy, another former homestay flew in from Hokkaido to see me and brought gifts for the kids. Like Masa, he is a real sweetheart.. We exchange letters at least once a year.

I'm sure this holiday was very educational for all of us. By this stage everyone was trying different foods and different activities. We had had an amazing vacation but we were all keen to go home.

A few things that linger in our minds are the plastic food set out in display cases near the restaurant doors so you could choose what you wanted even if you couldn't read the menu. Conveyer belts to move Sushi or to move cars. What next. Well next, maybe a fancy Japanese toilet like the one Motoko had. It even had a heated seat and oh so many control buttons. That would be a temptation for curious little kids.

Our take homes included two Japanese wedding Kimonos-one for Randi and one for Marcia. Randi's is very silvery and embroidered with wisteria and Marcia's is lined with red silk and embroidered with Cranes and pine boughs. These are family treasures. Marcia first saw hers when she was about thirteen. What a gift. I have it in my chest downstairs.

Chapter Twenty-five persons of interest

My daughters, Yvette and Nancy; homestays Vincent, Johnson, Frank and Ruby

Friends Susan, Lorena, Diana, Ellen and of course, BILL

Teachers Lori, Lucie, Rose, Sherry, Dan and Ralph my sister Susie

MY 60TH BIRTHDAY

CHAPTER TWENTY-SIX

BILL AND I

Nancy had set the date, invited the guests and decided she would put together a book to celebrate my 60th birthday. Besides she hosted the party. What follows is the contents of a book of treasures I was given. Yes, I know Yvette was pushing all her buttons from Portage La Prairie

Yes Sir,

"She's all that," just ask Wild Bill,

Yvette, Nancy, Ruby, Frank, Johnson, Vincent, Susan, Lorena, Diana,.......What do I think of when I think about my mom?

Christmas's and Birthday's, they were always so special. How?

Mom just had a knack for making them feel that way, real celebrations, where you felt special! Maybe it was a fancy cake she decorated herself, novelty items like blow your own free form balloons, fancy princess nightgowns, purple velvet shirts, skis that I couldn't find anywhere!! And believe me I looked, just like I did every year, boy she hid those well. [And I am much better now at not peeking, even when they come in boxes months early.] Surprise birthday parties prepared right under your nose….! I love birthdays and Christmases, and now even get to participate in unbirthdays, like Alice in Wonderland, and open houses, where I feel like such an honoured guest, when I visit with so many of our friends and relatives that I get to see so little of since I moved away, and I really cherish those times. She makes them possible.

She may be turning sixty, but even when you look at pictures of her past, even though she has white hair, I swear she is getting younger every day. She has more sparkle in her eye than ever. She loves life, her friends, and her family. She's a doer not just a talker. She's a teacher, opening people's minds, their eyes, getting them to look at things in new ways, teaching people to question, to think beyond what is obvious.

Roxsane, is an inspiration, travelling to distant places, taking up art-seriously-not just as an aside, writing on occasion, entering contests, stretching, reaching, growing…..

As a child we travelled by camper, and tent. We saw places few children see, homes built in mountainsides, shanty towns in Mexico, a raison factory, cheese factory, cotton fields, helicopter logging, desert sand storms…..she encouraged travel. When my sisters and I went off to Europe, backpacking at the ages of 16, 17 and 19, she said call me in a month so I know you are all right. A month! Now that's faith, and that was a trip I will never forget. In away I suppose, it was like a passage into being an adult. Knowing you could do it by yourself, you were ready to tackle the world.

My Mother, has gone through, mental and sexual abuse, she has gone through the death of her own child, through a divorce, and more. She has also, gone through happier times, the birth of her children, weddings, students, boarders, grandchildren, meeting Bill, living life. That is what she has chosen to do—Live Life to the Fullest.

I encourage her to continue, and I will watch and learn, and admire her strengths.

Remember, When we came to visit one summer.....first we stopped in Drumheller to check out the dinosaurs. While there, on the wall was the evolution of man. And Kelly and Kori, asked when were we monkeys? And I replied, "Oh, a very, very long time ago." They thought about that, and said, "So Grandma was a monkey before?" That was sure worth a chuckle, but now on thinking on it, maybe she still is.

Happy 60th!!!

Happy Birthday Mom,

Love from Yvette, Randi, Kori, Kelly and Allen

My Life With Roxsane   By Susan Cumberland

I first met Roxsane in 1983. She was out at UBC   studying her "konichiwa, arigato, and sumimasen". I went off to live in the "Land of the Rising Sun." While I was there I received a phone call from Roxsane as she was passing through. I didn't hear from her again until 1988 when I signed up for another Japanese class at UBC. There was Roxsane again. We struck up conversation and she invited me to her house for dinner. I learned of her life, her joys and her pain. I immediately recognized her strength, her energy, her compassion, her open mind and her sense of humour. I knew I had found a friend and a role model.

Roxsane ended up working with me at Dorset College for two years. I had the luxury of seeing her almost everyday. Then she went off to work in New Westminster High School.

In 1989, Roxsane and I were awarded bursaries by the BC Ministry of Education to study Japanese in Kobe, Japan. Off we went. Coincidentally our homestay families were out in the boondocks, but we were only a few blocks from each other. We rode bicycles to and from the train station in the humid, sweaty heat of Japan. It was mighty painful with a sake hangover, but we survived.

In 1995, I was living in San Diego and I was in charge of a short term English program for 250 Italians. I invited Roxsane down to teach. By the way, a gorgeous gentleman named Bill had entered Roxsane's life. Roxsane and Bill made their way to the US border with a Letter of Employment. The US officials didn't like the looks of the Canadian riff raffs and sent them back to Canuckville. I managed to contact the roughian US officials at the Blaine border crossing and sweet talk them into allowing these shady characters to enter the United States of America. A bit of rewording on the "Letter of Employment" helped.

While in San Diego, we took a trip to Tijuana. My friend, Georgina and I were waiting by the Mexican border for Roxsane and Bill [the two love birds] to show up. When they arrived they were in full colour. I mean FULL colour. Their outfits were bright orange, red, yellow, etc…..This flashy neon couple walked the full length of Revolution Street and somehow managed to not get picked up by the fashion police. Georgina and I didn't lose sight of them that day.

Here we are in year Y2K and Roxsane has entered another decade of her lifetime. From the sushi bars of Japan to the mariachi bands of Mexico I have enjoyed my relations with this incredible woman who is my friend, role model, and sometimes my personal psychologist. Cheers to Roxsane! I look forward to many, many more years of fun and friendship. Susan Cumberland.

ROXSANE

I met Roxsane in September 1984 in a French class at SFU. I was new to Vancouver and very naïve to the world.

My first thought of her was "What the heck is she doing in a 1ˢᵗ year French course?" This is, of course, because she was close to my own mother's age and I certainly couldn't picture my mother at University.

Then I got to know her.

We quickly became friends and she became someone I always sought for advice and companionship. She had a wealth of knowledge and was a lot of fun to boot.

My next thought of Roxsane was "Does this woman ever get tired? She would be doing things from morning til night- never wasting a moment. She is almost twice my age and can completely wear me out.

My next thought of Roxsane was "Is there anything this woman cannot do? She was buying houses, ripping them apart, putting them back together again, adding finishing touches, taking University courses, flying all over the world, teaching at a college..

I have learned from Roxsane that no matter what you endure in life, there is always a reason to stand up, start over and get the most that life has to offer. She has taught me to figure out what I want in life, focus all my energies on that and to have faith it will come.

I look at Roxsane now and see how far she has come in the fifteen years I have known her. She has two children, five grandchildren, a partner she is in love with and lots of friends—all who respect and love her.

My current thoughts of Roxsane are that "she is an amazing person, someone I will always admire and look up to, hope that I can achieve half of what she has achieved in life, hope that I can give back to her

what she has given to me and hope that we will always be friends.
Lorena

A SISTER'S POINT OF VIEW

Memories are such that each and everyone of us perceives, the events of our lives in our own special way. Thru all the years of sisterhood we have traveled far and learned about each other with out our rose coloured glasses on at times. At these times we have met our match in many ways and the one we love at the same time. We are original and yet the same at times, we have come from the same parents enjoyed the same family, events and outings and are still ourselves.

Some of the events we have shared have enlightened our hearts and others our emotions or intellect.

Roxsane and I have shared the joys of our children and the challenges which they have given us, in which we grow stronger, more loving and understanding. We have shared the joys of marriage as well as the difficulties in their passing. A lot has been learned by these events and we are better people and friends because of these sharings.

I would like to thank Roxsane for some of the experiences she has brought and shared with me.

Girl Guide Camp "Serendipity" an international experience on many levels. The wonderful women we met and whom we shared our lives for weeks under canvas. We were all headed in the same direction, to bring experiences and hopefullu more unity and peace to the world in our lifetime or at least to leave it a little better off for us having visited here.

Golf!! Who plays that silly game? Who in their right mind would wander around in the rain chasing a little white ball? We would!! Its great fun and we need more of that in our lives today. We've learned to challenge ourselves, no "beat each other" just better our own score if we can. Also to enjoy each others company and chats over a game or the tea or the goodies after. I think we will always be playing golf, even if not together or on the greens, so much fun we have together!!!!

And of course those self help books and those physic experiences!! Never a dull moment in our lives. We have had so much to talk about as we get to know ourselves better and to know each other. One can only know we are working hard at being our selves.

Like I say we are original and yet the same.!!

I love you Roxsane for all the wonderful times and talks we have enjoyed. I know we will be doing this for years to come, so settle in and enjoy this year as we will be busy for a lot more getting to know each other better.

Remember to always be whom you are which will help me know who I am too. Love you lots.

One of your favorite sisters!!!!

To Roxsane, We teachers all agree: Roxsane Rocks! [But never the boat] We wish to express our greatest admiration and cheer for your birthday.

Thank you, for you.

Verse 1.

There once was a team called
The mob
Who were stripped of their function
By Bob
"Never mind" said Roxsane
"I'll do what I can"
and proceeded to teach ESL, CAPP

and Co-op

Verse 2

There once was a super lady
Named Roxsane
Who always does much more than
Anyone else can
She's forever in motion
Not without some commotion
And slowing down will never be
Part of her plan

Verse 3

There is a dynamite
Dragon
Whose heart is too big
For a wagon
She works and she plays
Says everythings Okay
Then leaves everyone else
Laggin'

Verse 4

There once was a lady
Next door
Who created and painted
Galore
Her deeds artistic
Were simply fantastic
That everyone begged
For more.

Verse 5

There was a bright lady
Of New West
Who often came to work
In a vest
Her fashion design
Was always divine
That everyone quoted
It's the best.

Verse 6

There once was a lady,
Soon sixty
Whose name is Roxsane
And not Dixie
She's smily and smart
And has such a big heart,
We wish her the best
And sweet sixty
Love from Lori, Rose,Lucie, Sherry, Dan, and Ralph

Roxsane - Happy Birthday!

Roxsane - the name must mean, "The one who goes beyond..."

Roxsane has always been exceptional in her accomplishments.

Not just Grade XI and XII, but also Grade XIII in two years, and not just school, but flower designing at Royal City Florists on Saturdays, which meant early mornings at bus stops.

Teaching school, not in the Lower Mainland, no, but up Harrison Lake two hours!
Moving back a little closer, to Sardis now, the mother of not one (like me), but three precious little girls, all in a row!

Over the years in Squamish, a houseful of projects, sewing and artwork, not just by Mom, but all the girls, too!

Girl Guides, not just local activities, of which there were plenty, but International Camps, Headquarters and Conferences.

Later still, buying and remodelling not just one but several houses, and not just buying and contracting tradesmen, but personally repairing and restoring them, which raised their value significantly.

Always taking courses, not one, but six, sometimes all at once...
Must learn to swim, take a course. Not just locally, drive for two hours to get there!

Needed Spanish, take a course. Need Japanese, not just a little awareness, travelled to Japan and then taught there!

Made contacts in several south Asian countries on other travels, not just for personal enhancement, but which assisted greatly in marketing international programs for the School District.

Not just making good friends on her holidays, but inviting them back, some to stay for years! Many students have called Roxsane's home their home.
She learned their ways and their foods, some of their languages.

Always learning. *Lifelong Learning*, is a phrase today, and Roxsane has lived it all her life.

Take courses! Take a degree. Drive all the way up Burnaby Mountain to SFU for weeks and months! Study something exotic, like the economic situation for women in Russia.

Learn to dance! Learn to golf! Learn the nuances of photography. Roxsane - a Time Management Phenomenon!

Roxsane, not only keeping a home, cooking for Bill and students and

herself, being a Mom and a Grandma, but teaching full time, and marking student assignments at home, but also producing not just one or two, but a gallery full of marvelous tissue collages, called Chigiri-e.

As I write, I'm on a Greyhound Bus travelling from Kamloops, passing snow covered trees, snowy rocks in the streams, snow-covered houses and fences. If Roxsane were here, in her mind she'd be designing a Chigiri scene in muted tones.

Roxsane has learned about gardening, and roofs and wiring, plumbing, glasswork, and constructing an addition to her house, so that she is able to supervise

construction workers.
Yvette and Nancy, also involved, have learned all these skills, and it's no surprise that their careers include many creative ventures, architecture and construction designing.

Then there's the allergy problem. Not just one item, but countless challenges to the system. Not just for herself, but her daughters, also.

Roxsane has made time in her life for her family, her neighbours, her friends, her students and colleagues, and her sweetheart.
Time to work and time to play. Time to clean and cook, but also time to create, and time for herself.

Roxsane, a very special person to admire, a person to love.
Happy 60th Birthday, dear Roxsane, dear friend.

With love always, and many encouragements for new ventures, your friend for around 45 years,

Ellen

IN THE BEGINNING...

One Friday night in late August of 1992, I reluctantly decided to attend a singles dance held in a church at 49th and Oak Street. I paid my five-dollar entry fee, received a number and sauntered off to a corner facing the entrance, cursing the fates that had brought me there. I felt like a two-time loser, having first been widowed and second been divorced.

While ruminating in the attic of my mind, I spotted a pretty, petite, curly-haired lady clad in leotards, short skirt and a sweater. Her appearance seemed at odds with her attire, a fiftyish face in a youthful ensemble. My curiousity was piqued by her shapely figure, especially her sculptured bottom. "She looks interesting," I thought to myself, even though she had come with a male companion who somehow didn't fit the picture.

At this particular dance a discussion preceded the dancing. Holding our numbers, we were dispersed to various rooms accompanied by a facilitator, who by coincidence or fate, happened to be Roxsane. During the discussion, Roxsane's escort constantly tried to monopolize the conversation. She frequently had to calm down his outbursts.

I wondered how such an attractive, intelligent lady could be associated with such a loonie. After our discussion period, I wandered over to the bar, picked up a glass of apple juice and watched the dancers as the music began. Feeling rather melancholy and ambivalent, I contemplated leaving. Suddenly I was confronted by my beautiful, blue-eyed Roxsane. "Would you like to dance?" she asked. Well, I thought, if she had the courage to ask how could I deny a damsel in distress?

We glided onto the dance floor in silence. After the dance, I found a seat and struck up a conversation with another man. Later that same night, Roxsane appeared before me requesting a second dance. Again, I acquiesced. After our dance, I departed for home early.

Two weeks later, same dance, same lady asking to dance. But this time, we began to get acquainted between dances. I found out that her male friend was just a tenant and that she was a teacher. During our conversation, I sensed her attraction for me. However, I was still unsure of my feelings.

The rest is history. Teachers have a fondness for little Johnnys, you know. Friendship blossomed into love. A dinner invitation, a warm fire built by Johnson who then discreetly disappeared, an invitation to get cozy by the fireplace, a first kiss and my fate was sealed. The wily trout was in the canny angler's net.

TODAY

Together we have surmounted all the obstacles strewn in our path and have forged an inspired enduring love based on acceptance, truth, humour and kindness. Roxsane, you fill my days with sunshine and my nights with ecstasy.

As an added bonus, our adult children choose to be friends. I now have two more beautiful daughters and five lively grandchildren. Thank you! Truly, my cup runneth over. Happy 60th birthday, my love!

Dear Roxsane and Bill   *Dec.13, 00*

First of all I'll celebrate your 60th, too. "Happy Birthday to You". I think you seem to be more active than before. I was so surprised to see the sample art you sent me. When did you start painting? They are like professional ones. What a great! You had an award of excellence at FCA. How nice! You deserve it, I'm sure. How did you polish your sense of paintings? Paintings make you relax? Are you going to get a show in Japan, or other countries? Is that one of your dreams? I hope it'll come true as soon as possible.

I like "Spring is Here" of the samples. Because colours used in the painting are springy for me and the atmosphere is easy. I'd like to sit back and relax there for days. I love that painting. Please hang in there.

My family are fine. My husband and daughter are working. My son is now a student of a vocational school after graduation of University. His dream is to work at a airport. He likes airplanes. I'm,also a student of National University Graduate school. I went there right after the graduation of Kobe City University this March. I major in the Education for the Handicapped. Mainly I learn psycology and counseling there. Just a week ago we had a presentation for ten minutes each student in front of some professers in order to take advice or instruction from them. It was a hard time for us. I had butterflies in my stomach. So did most students I'm studying about school refusal, which means students who don't go to school, refuse to go to school, can't go to school because of bullying or other reasons. This year the number of that is over 130,000 including elementary, junior, senior high school students in Japan. This problem is increasingly a big social issue year by year. I'm interested in them. But study in graduate school is tougher than I've thought. Almost every day I go to school by car. It takes over 1 hour one way or I have to attend some study sessions. It's a busy life for me than I thought. I've less time to study English than before. I wonder if you have truancy in school like in Japan. I heard that home schooling is popular in the US. In Japan, not so popular now though, there are some students among truant students. It might catch on. Anyway there are a lot of parents, especially mothers who suffer from it. Today it's very cold here in Japan.

Your friend E K

Chapter twenty-six persons of interest
Randi and I
Nancy's Architecture friends Yaz, Andy and their children.
The Graeme Johnstone family in Leeds Francis Boag in Aberdeen
Our Yorkshire tour guide in Whitby Ina, Jan, Nikolaj and Amanda
Diana and Jorma, Marikri, and Ville in Turku, Finland
Bertile and Jean Champarnaud in Aix-en –Provence
Diana's cousin in Barcelona Annie {the French Teacher at NWSS]
and her husband Dave in France.

CHAPTER TWENTY-SEVEN

2002 RANDI AND I EXPLORE EUROPE

Can you imagine a more unlikely pair of backpacking travellers than a fifteen year old, lively, young woman, and her 62 year old grandmother—me? Randi's Mom, Yvette and her aunt Nancy both gave Randi the same advice "Don't forget to feed the Dragon." Yvette did the research to make sure we didn't miss anything important. Our family put together a list of people who might put us up for a night or two, who might help us wherever we ended up.

We landed in Gatwick, outside of London, took the train to Picadilly Circus, then took the tube to Yaz and Andy's place. These were folks who had worked in Architecture with Nancy. They had two children Nina and Sam. We rested up, got acquainted with Yaz who was busy getting the children's supper. Her Dad dropped by to see his grandchildren and to help keep them busy while Yaz made a delicious creamy soup of yams, red peppers and spices. We adjusted to the time change and planned the next day's highlights of London by bus. We bussed past Big Ben, the Parliament Buildings, Trafalgar Square, to Covent Gardens where we got off and explored the many shops. We were having a snack when a very talented African woman started singing an Aria from Bizet's Carmen. She was impressive. However, the highlight of our time in London turned out to be shopping in Harrod's. There we were lost in the crowds. We marveled at the choices in the food floor. We poked here and there and found a brochure on a display of dresses worn by Princess Di and another for a display of tiaras. As we were heading out to go home to Yaz and Andy's we stopped at a jewelry counter with many pieces on sale. One was a gorgeous waterfall of silver-a necklace Randi had to have for her Mother. I said "No way. This is our first day. I don't want to carry around anything that expensive. It will get lost too easily. No, this is ridiculous." But she prevailed. I said "I can pay for it but you have to carry it and keep it safe." She did.

I remember when Randi was two and a half walking to a friend's house with her. It was "this way Grandma. No, Grandma, this way." So it was on our forty-six days abroad. Only once did she get confused. In London she took us to change money following directions from Yaz. I would have taken the bus on the wrong side of the street and gone who knows where. She made sure we caught all the correct trams and buses and I was so glad she had come with me. I didn't factor in the left/right changes as easily. We had our Britrail passes activated so our next stop was York. We sorted our plans on the train. Had lunch when we got to York. We checked out the minster with its beautiful interior, its carved choir lofts, its immensity. Off to the Shambles where the quaint style, the tiny shops with such charm and diverse products could have kept us busy for a long time but time was important, we had people to meet before supper and that meant another train journey so we left to climb the Roman walls around the city. We checked the time for the train to Leeds and caught part of an afternoon concert outside near the station. We thoroughly enjoyed York.

The Johnstone family met us at the station in Leeds. They are friends of Randi's other Grandmother. Randi and the two girls exchanged ideas and shared teenage habits and concerns. I was amazed at how compact British homes are and how much Art they collected. These people were very generous. We spent a lot of time talking about our climates, the cultural differences and our families. The next day they took us to a restaurant that served OODLES OF NOODLES. We all ordered our favorites from an extensive menu. The food was delicious. We parted promising to keep in touch and we did for a few years.

Aberdeen, Scotland is where Francis Boag, an artist I'd seen featured in the International Artists Magazine lives. I'd contacted him from home and set up a meeting so he met us at the train. He drove us around Aberdeen, took us to see his studio-- check out his colorful landscapes on line. I was keen to learn how he organizes his work. Then he took us for lunch and put us back on the train heading for Inverness. What a kind, thoughtful gentleman Artist.

ELGIN MARBLES

Apparently the hostel in Inverness has a resident ghost but we didn't see it. I believe some of the Elgin marbles were there, too. We wandered around the area taking in the different house styles, the layout of the countryside and got enough exercise so we could sit on the train going through Perth to Edinburgh the next day. We arrived mid-afternoon, checked into the hostel, then explored the area close to the hostel. We were starving so we took advantage of a café serving baked potatoes with various stuffings as their speciality. We ordered the baked bean ones. They were delicious, quite different from our baked beans.

RANDI IN WHITBY WITH THE
YORKSHIRE LADY AND FRIEND

In the morning I had a headache, a head cold, and very little energy so after leaving the hostel I found a spot where I could sit in the sunshine, babysit our luggage, and let Randi go see what she could of Edinbugh castle. The train we took next was going through Berwick upon Tweed to Newcastle where we switched lines to a more local line into Whitby. Whitby is the seaport Captain Cook left from. It is very hilly. There were many boats in the harbour--some rigged with full sail to accommodate tourists. We climbed up the hill to the hostel, and met a couple of English ladies one from Yorkshire. [I've been told my father's ancestors came from there.\ The Brits were eager to show us the town. We all piled into the

Yorkshire lady's car. We had a glorious afternoon,and evening exploring the back streets, the harbor, and their favorite nooks and crannies. We had supper together; explored the cemetery, and shared our previous adventures before turning in for the night.

MUMMERS IN YORK

Next we headed for Bath. We'd been on the train too long, and carrying our luggage made me opt to sit out with the luggage while Randi explored. We briefly discussed staying the night, but I wanted to get to Betty Millin's as our Britrail pass would expire in a couple of days. I tried phoning. No answer. We had said we would probably not arrive till the next day. I kept trying,every time the train stopped. We got into Haslemere about 6pm. Phoned. Had supper. Phoned. Explored. Phoned and finally at 8:30 decided to head for London hoping for a hostel. No luck. We headed from London to Canterbury and got off. It turned out to be graduation night. Every place was full. We headed back to the station. It was locked. We had come in on the last train.

Oh my God, what a night. Fortunately it was not raining hard. We wandered around staying not for from the station. We had our luggage to contend with. After some time I decided we would try to sleep in a stairwell bend leading down to a parking area for a complex of middle class flats. It seemed all the people were already asleep. Sleep, well,… no, not well. We shifted positions often. Finally shortly after 5am, we collected our gear, and set off to walk some of the Roman walls. Looking back at the city shrouded in the morning mists is one of Randi's favorite memories.

We caught the first train to Dover. I can't remember what we had for breakfast or even if we had breakfast.

We took the boat to Ostende, Belgium and validated our Eurrail passes on arrival asking the agent to book us through to Fredrikshavn. He did. I phoned Ina, my friend who had worked with me in Mexico, and told her we would arrive at 7:15 pm. We boarded the train knowing we needed to change trains in Hamburg. By the time we arrived there, we had learned that there were two Fredrikshavns one on the extreme south of Germany and the one we wanted in the very north of Denmark. In order to solve the ticket mess I left Randi on the train platform with our luggage. I spent the next two hours in line-ups with not so helpful ticket agents. Fortunately, Randi waited patiently.

RANDI, INA AND AMANDA
WITH SCULPTURE

We got our tickets sorted, got on the next train to Denmark which put us on a local train at midnight as we crossed into Denmark. The train was very crowded, very slow. People were sleeping in the aisles. There was luggage everywhere. Every time you got comfortable the train would stop to let off or accept passengers. We got to Fredrikshavn around 7am. We enquired at two or three shops how to get to Horsengade 27 and finally walked there. Ina had been angry as we hadn't shown up the night before. She had made a fancy spread and even met a later train. We were just worn out after all the ups and downs of the past few days. Ina, Jan, Nikolaj and Amanda made us feel at home.

We rested, toured the beaches of the North Sea. I can remember all the jellyfish, loads of them. We checked out the local museums and Art places. We walked and talked remembering times when Ina was my assistant at Our Cabana in Mexico as well as when I had visited just before Ina and Jan's wedding in 1988. Many things had changed. Ina was teaching Grade 3 or 4 at the time. Jan was engrossed in his Navy career, Nikolaj was starting high school, Amanda was eleven or twelve, I think.

After a couple of days rest Randi and I booked passage to Oslo. Once there we checked into a youth hostel. Randi wasn't feeling well so rather than trying to fit in too many side trips we decided to spend a day relaxing at Vigeland sculpture Park. We bought picnic food, took something to sit on, wore our jackets and rested or explored the park at will. The sculptures are amazing showing every stage of life--the sad worn laborers, the mischievous children teasing each other and couples in love. What we didn't understand were the many crocodiles or alligators. What was the sculptor saying? Were they our ancestors? Or predators or just a form that fascinated the sculptor?

IN VIGELAND SCULPTURE PARK, OSLO

Randi was up to seeing Oslo the next day so we checked out the Norse Folk Museum and a couple of other sites before booking the night train to Stockholm.

In the morning we booked into the hostel near the Wasa where Jan, Ina and I had stayed in 1988. That day we poked into many shops and cafes in Old Town Stockholm.

In the morning we boarded the ferry to Turku, Finland.

Finland was one of the highlights of our trip. My friend, Diana met us at the ferry and took us to their home in Vahdontie. Diana had already set up the display of my Art in the local library. I had shipped it earlier by DHL. In Diana's eyes I was a celebrity. I did a Chigiri-e workshop that was well attended when I was there. One of the women did an exquisite piece of little soft, puffy flowers blowing in the wind. I was so lucky to have Diana to translate for me. Diana was a friend from Mexico City. She was very active in the Guias [Mexican Girl Guides]. She was sent to a major World Association of Girl Guides and Girl Scouts Conference in Nairobi, Kenya. From there she had gone on to a camp somewhere in Europe [maybe Germany] where she met her future husband, Jorma.

DIANA AND I top   FINNISH FRIENDS bottom

His sisters were there, too. I think she went to Finland to meet his family. I know Jorma went to Mexico to meet the Berber family before they were married. They were great hosts. Jorma has a factory where he uses his engineering skills. Both Jorma and Diana speak English adding Finnish and Spanish to the mix. Diana was teaching Spanish at the University. The children Ville and Kristina [Marikri] kept Randi busy learning their games and hobbies. We even went out to their cabin and went fishing. We met their grandmother and Aunts who were also involved in Guiding or Scouting. We learned that "Hey' could mean hello or good-bye or ??? something like "ciao" in Italian.

SILJA FERRY,   RANDI ON THE STOCKHOLM BRIDGE

There was a Renaissance Fair in town so we took that in. Randi and Marikri took part in sack races and walking on stilts. We ate huge sausages wrapped in lettuce leaves and poked our noses in anywhere something of interest caught our eye. We preferred to stay with the Berber/Raiko family rather than to go to Helsinki. Now Diana has five of my paintings. She sent the rest of them back to me by DHL and I squared up with Diana for the shipping costs. Our visit was about one week long. We were sad to leave but Diana had passed on contacts in Barcelona and Aix-en-Provence which made our lives so much easier.

We took the ferry back to Stockholm and continued our journey south to Mainz in Germany by Eurail. In Mainz I bought parts to make a new doll similar to one I had given Randi when she was three. This time I wanted a man's head and wig so I could make a mischievous Irish imp. Once I had all the pieces I needed we headed for Rothenburg ob der Tauber, an amazingly well preserved medieval town. It is very much a liederhosen, gingersnap, rustic tourist's town. Even McDonald's had a medieval type sign. We wandered the cobblestone streets and the town square. The timber framed buildings, red roofs and beefy fortifications make it an impressive tourist attraction. They sell Schneeballs, [snowballs] deep fried like doughnuts and covered with fancy confections. Very filling.

Next stop Fussen in beautiful Bavaria. There we joined a tour to Neuschwanstein castle, the one that inspired Disney's Fantasy castle. Inside the finished rooms are elegant masterpieces fit for the King but much of the castle hasn't been completed yet. The castle is at the very top of a cliff so you can survey all of the kingdom.

Fussen itself is a very tidy town with hanging baskets, window boxes with red geraniums and an elaborate clock tower. We checked the shops out looking for a peasant blouse for Randi. We didn't find exactly what she wanted. However the aroma of freshly baked bread lured us into an outdoor café. The food was delicious. We left stuffed.

Venice was our next destination. On the train in the night there was a scuffle as we crossed the border from Switzerland to Italy. The border police removed a male passenger. He resisted to no avail. The officials checked our passports at least twice. I was shocked as no one had checked our passports since we validated our Eurail passes. We didn't get much sleep that night.

Arriving in Venice we stored our luggage. We threaded our way through the side streets, over bridges, gawking at Carnival masks, checking for souvenirs. We took a vaporeto across the canal only to find no room at the hostel. While there we booked a space in the hostel at the nearby town, Veneto. We went looking for supper and walked into an Italian café. We had a hard time getting service. Seems they didn't speak or understand English. I ordered Spaghetti con Funji. I figured that meant mushrooms. We did get supper but I think they were relieved and happy when we paid for dinner and left.

Murano with its beautiful glass work beckoned. Chihully, the Washington State glass artist, had a pathway installation of his sublime glass creations. Awesome. We took lots of photos. Our purchases were pendants and earrings. Often they were cheaper back in Venice itself. Burano was next. This area is famous for cutwork and embroidery. I bought a small cutwork embroidered umbrella for my youngest grand daughter—a prized possession.

We hoped to book a hostel in Southern France but the staff in the Veneto hostel said there were no openings anywhere.

Out came plan B. Randi had to use her French. Imagine someone you've never even heard of calling and saying "you don't know me but a friend of your cousin said you might let us stay with you for a couple of days. My Grandma knows your cousin, too. If it's all right we will arrive tomorrow afternoon."

Bertile tried to make sense of it all. She asked Randi to phone from the station when we arrived. Randi did. But she called from the high speed train station and Bertile went to the local one. Randi gave her a description of us and Bertile told her, "I'm short and fat." She isn't.

We waited and waited. Eventually Bertile flew down the platform to find us. She had asked at the old station. Thank God. She whisked us to her home, introduced us to Jean, her husband. The she asked if we would like to come to an Artist friend's opening. Of course, we did. We enjoyed the Art, the hors d' oeuvres and Randi was given wine she thought was apple juice. My French is shabby, imperfectly pronounced and liable to get me into trouble so Randi was in charge. Back at Bertile's she explained they were going to a retirement party the next evening. "Would we like to come along?"

"Sure, can we contribute some money for the gas and the gift?" We had an interesting time at the party. Randi talked and I listened to the fellows manning the barbeque. Bertile and Jean visited their friends. We had travelled a long ways to a place near Hyeres.

The Champarnaud's quaint cottage had a large yard with roosters strutting around. The currant bushes were suffering from an invasion of white shelled snails. Pretty to look at but…. We discussed our journey, Bertile's Artwork and mine, her cousin Karen in Puebla, Mexico, our friend Diana in Finland, where else we were going, our families, and, and. Bertile took us to the market in Aix-en-Provence. Another memory to treasure. Bertile and Jean said "You must have Cassoulet for supper when you are in Carcassone." We took their advice.

Carcassone is the magnificent medieval walled castle where we saw knights on horseback jousting. It is a showcase of medieval military architecture. We walked the walls, took in the views from the top and thoroughly enjoyed the cassoulet, a rich man's version. Randi's great grandmother made a more humble cassoulet mainly of navy beans with onions and bacon for flavoring. Both delicious.

The next day we ate at McDonald's where the burger was served in a foccasia bun, a change we didn't find in any other McDonald's.

SOME OF GAUDI'S CREATIONS

We phoned Diana's cousin who met us shortly after we arrived in Barcelona. They took us to their apartment, explaining how to care for it and where to put the key when we left. Then we went for dinner. Later they drove us around the harbor and up the hill to see the lights. How beautiful it was. Then they were off.

On our own we made breakfast, got the metro schedule, browsed around our area learning the bus stops and grocery shops. By noon we were at Parc Guell with its whimsical salamander, colorful tile mosaic benches, and its tunnel like walkways. Everywhere you could see spires of flowing natural shapes decorated with wasted ceramic pieces. It is a magical place. After supper we walked along Las Ramblas enjoying the many street performers, kiosks selling flowers, and snacks. Las Ramblas is almost always crowded.

We took transit to the Fundacio Joan Miro, a world class museum. I've always been attracted to his playful creations. On our way back we stopped at the Sagrada Familia church that has been being built for decades and decades. I love the tree like pillars whose branches hold up the roof, the sunflower designs, the carefully tinted stained glass windows and the odd grotesque piece that brings you back to reality. I hope they continue working on the completion of this mind-boggling structure. About this time I noticed symptoms of a Kidney infection so we went to a farmacia, I asked for some Keflex and got the drug to fight the infection. I wish it was that easy here.

In the morning we tidied up, packed our bags and headed for the train to Paris. We got on but I didn't realize there was a time change at the border so we didn't get the couchettes we had ordered as we missed our connection. Darn. We arrived in Paris a few hours late. We phoned Annie and Dave, our hosts who were house sitting fifteen minutes past Versailles and got specific directions. They met us at the station. We had bought our Paris Metro passes before heading to meet Annie and Dave. We were very lucky to have such generous friends.

The next day was rainy. The lines to get in the Louvre were long. We stood in the rain for about an hour and a half before we got in. Most of the Art work was very old. Yes, they were beautifully done but one gets tired of still life and battle scenes. With the crowds you couldn't get close to the Mona Lisa. We saw her from a distance and decided to leave. We walked to Notre Dame Cathedral. Checked out the boats along the river and went back to Annie and Dave.

When we went to the D'Orsay museum it was almost the same— lining up in the rain to see what we had seen in textbooks, fighting the crowds at the featured exhibits and leaving disappointed. We tried to find the fashion areas, checked out L'Arc de Triomphe and the Eiffel tower. This time we got off and explored Versailles on our way back. A stunning, opulent interior, so much gold, the tapestries, elegance everywhere. It's beauty is overwhelming. The gardens fade off to the distance but the main section with its ponds and curlicues is a tribute to perfection. Mind boggling!

Randi was adamant. "I do not want to go back to Paris." So we talked it over with Annie and Dave, and decided we'd all hop in their car, and drive out into the country. We had a wonderful time. We shopped in the local boulangerie [bakery] for meat pies, eclairs, and baguettes to take home. We had a picnic lunch, saw examples of architecture designed by Mies Van Der Rohe, and meandered through the farming areas enjoying being away from the city. I guess we were missing being home. After all Randi lived on a half section [320 acre] farm in Portage la Prairie, Manitoba [population 14,000]. We were ready to head to Amsterdam, and HOME.

DAVE, ANNIE, RANDI AND I, ROOFTOPS OF AMSTERDAM.

We were so well cared for. We thanked Annie and Dave. Took our gear, and caught the fast train to Amsterdam. We found a place in a hostel in the Red Light District. We traipsed up, and down the canals, enjoyed the tree lined streets, took in the Van Gogh Museum, our favorite, of course, and the Rijksmuseum. We went out to see a few windmills, found a couple of Art studios, and continued to search for the peasant blouse Randi wanted. On our last day, we found an open air market. Randi was sorting through a jumble of clothes,when the peasant blouse appeared. I was choosing some socks, my usual take home. We happily left the market, but for the first time Randi's sense of direction got skewed. We were not heading to the station as planned. I had to ask two or three people to get us on track. As I was tensing up, Randi remembered the last words of her Mom and her Aunt "always feed the Dragon", so we found a snack bar. We checked our timing for trains to the airport the following day; headed to the hostel, and packed for home. We had learned a lot about each other, and ourselves. When we went for Vegan DimSum a couple of weeks back, she told me she still wears her peasant blouse.

By the way, at fifteen, Randi had saved her earnings to pay for her trip. The only things I paid for were the hostels, and such in Skandinavia as they are very costly. We keep up with each other's achievements, and travels.

Opening of Eileen Fong Co-Op Gallery in Tinseltown

Chapter twenty seven persons of interest
Just me, Ginny, Marj., Kathy, Gary, Judy, Rob, Olga, SiPei, Grace

CHAPTER TWENTY-EIGHT

BECOMING AN ARTIST

In 1976 I studied Drawing, Painting Acrylics, Spinning, Dyeing, Fabric Design and Soft Sculpture at Capilano College in their Squamish location. In 1984 I learned how to create pictures using torn Japanese washii paper in Japan. I bought some paper and brought it back to Canada. .I didn't use it until Yvette asked me to make her a thirty by forty inch picture similar to Bergsma's River of Tulips to put in her living room. I took up the challenge, bought myself a roll of paper that I taped to the living room picture window. I cut, tore and glued the pieces in place. Fortunately I had bought several sheets of random pink dyed washii paper. I completed the piece in a couple of weeks, and shipped it in a tube. She had it framed. It hung behind her couch for years.

Doing that picture was the shove that I needed to really get into Art. I enjoyed working with that paper. In short order I made a picture of striking mountains using a photo from National Geographics—a No –No, so that was donated to a charity as a fund raiser. After that I relied on my own photos or just my creativity. I made a piece called BLUE LAKE and another called EVENSONG both sold at the opening of my first solo show in 2000 at Queen's Park Gallery as did THE BIRCHES and a few others. People were really impressed. Someone went home and phoned their artist friend [a professional!]. He and his wife arrived a few minutes before closing. He stayed upstairs carefully checking each individual piece.. He wore glasses, so he would take them off, look at the picture, put them on, look at the picture, stand back eight or so feet, look at the picture, move in until he was inches from the glass. Then he called his wife . He suggested buying a picture of irises. "No, " said his wife. "come down here. You need to see the trees." They bought them. They said they would never look at paper the same way again.

Top Workshop in Portage La Prairie Bottom at Creative Framing, Grp4Art
JUDY, ROB, ROXSANE, KATHY, GARY, GINNY maybe Marj took the photo?

In 2000 I was juried in as an active member of the FCA Federation of Canadian Artists. I won an Award of Excellence for FRUTERIA, an experimental piece in the Millenium Show. That September, I joined the Burnaby Artists Guild after being on the waiting list for two years. The group had a balanced mix of people, some very talented, capable; a few came for the social time; others to learn all they could to enable them to create the pieces they envisioned. The group was open to all. If you made it past the waiting list you were in. I made friends and by the Annual General Meeting the next May, I became the treasurer. A year or two later, I became the President and remained so until 2014 when I moved back to being treasurer.

One of the reasons people join the Guild, is so they have a chance to sell their work. We have two sales each year, one in late March or early April, the other just before Hallowe'en. Before every sale we get a few calls asking to be able to show and sell. Then I have to explain the rules—you must be a paid member, attend two business meetings and three other meetings between shows, buy a ten dollar book of raffle tickets, work a couple of shifts at the sale, and pay to rent the space you need. Getting ready for a show takes a lot of work, The show committee works very hard. Fortunately our shows are very popular.

OLGA AND I at Port Moody Show
SIPEI, ROXSANE AND GRACE at EMMELLE'S

Being in the Guild helped six of us to work together as THE GROUP OF SIX. Ginny had been asked to show her work at the Raquet Club and she wanted support. The six of us were pleased to be showing together so we searched for other venues, other opportunities. We were five women and one man but after being together for a few years Gary, an ex-military photographer went in for his annual physical, had a stroke and never came home. A year or so later Judy who was the vice president of the Guild and a Group of Six member, moved to the Courtenay/Comox area on Vancouver Island In November. She was healthy or so we thought but in May she died from breast cancer. She had been in remission for years. What a loss. Our group was not Six anymore. Looking for a new name Kathy came up with Grp4Art and that works for us. Ginny, Marj, Kathy and I hang cooperative showings of our diverse efforts. We paint together frequently and always can find helpful critics when needed.

Sometimes I lead but I, also follow. Eileen Fong, a very prolific, talented Artist has been a mentor for me. Like her I have joined the North Vancouver Arts Council; the Arts Council of Surrey; the New Westminster Arts Council, even the Richmond Arts Council. I keep my Federation of Canadian Artists, Burnaby Arts Council and Surrey Art Gallery Association memberships up to date, too. Both Eileen and I have work available for rental through North Van and Surrey Art Rental systems.

In 2002 I sent my Art to Turku, Finland. My friend, Diana, arranged for it to be displayed in the local library and for me to give a chigiri-e workshop to people there. Fortunately Diana was available as a translator. In Canada I have given workshops in Portage la Prairie, Manitoba; Steveston, Abbotsford, South Delta and other Greater Vancouver locations. Chigiri-e workshops can be arranged.

I try to get my work juried into upcoming shows whenever I can. I have been represented in over seventy juried shows and won a few awards.

My favorite solo show was called "Creations of an Elastic Mind" I am an experimental artist. One day I picked up part of a metal template—a discard or whatever and put it on my classroom desk. Students who came up for whatever reason usually shook their head but said nothing. One said,"Mrs. Tiernan why don't you throw away that garbage?" "I'm going to use it in my art. "No, --it isn't anything." Well, I took it home and it became an important feature of a piece I call "Industrial Gold" an abstract assemblage that would suit an engineer's office. Possibly they would understand the meaning of "Industrial Gold" the clarity of the message I was trying to send.

I like to try new approaches-maybe not new to others but new to me when I am working on an intuitive piece. For instance a quinacridone gold underpainting on a sheet of warercolour paper that I decide to play with blues and greens directed uncontrollably by saran wrap or wax paper both crumpled just to see what would happen. The journey continued when I discovered an insect chewn columbine stock in the back garden. The green was so perfectly etched by pale yellow outlining the missing parts. I was fascinated by the rare beauty of the destruction. On the gold background I used a piece of a heavy lace border fabric to imprint a column on the right with much narrower dark brown strips to emphasize the height. Then I added a sketch of the columbine stem, a little to the left. The random patterns of the blues and greens led to an unpredictable growth of flowers-rusts, oranges, and whites and their foliage, all dictated by the patterns from the saran wrap making this an unusual piece of work. I really enjoy the places my imagination takes me. I am open to using whatever is at hand.

I believe in life long learning so credit must be given to the Artists whose workshops I have attended. The first one I took was taught by Donna Baspaly, an amazing local Artist .I really admire her style. After that I usually took a workshop coordinated by Mary Stewart in Naniamo most summers. Workshop leaders were American Masters including Betsy Dillard-Stroud; Carole Barnes; Pat Dews; Robert Burridge; Maureen Briolette; Steven Aimone; and Annie Morgan. Each of them taught me to push my boundaries, try whatever might work and keep learning anytime from anyone. I try to pass that along whenever I give a workshop. At this point in my life I give Chigiri-e workshops for Opus Art supplies in their Granville Island shop and in their Coquitlam one as well. They are usually well attended.

In 1989 I wrote and self published CELEBRATE JAPAN a book on the annual festivals the Japanese celebrate. It sold over 2500 copies. I am currently waiting for my book of Art and Poetry ART AND SOUL to be published. I, also wrote a memoir of the first fifty years of my life called "ZIP". This book ZIPPING ALONG is about the second section of my life. It ends in 2003 with my retirement.

Dear Roxsane,   December 14, 2002

Thanks a lot for your Christmas letter. Whenever I read your annual letter, I admire you and your way of living as you seem to step up year by year. You've become an excellent artist now. I was also impressed that you have a lot of friends almost all over the world. You're like a cosmopolitan! How gorgeous your wandering around Europe with Randi was! She must have been your great help. I think she might be about 16 years old. The trip was surely a kind of adventure and it gave you great opportunities to made new friends as you said in your letter. I love Gaudi, too, so I flew to Spain with my daughter Mari four years ago and visited Sagrada Familia in Barcelona. I went to Madrid, Toledo, Seville, Cordoba and Granada. I was very moved by the architecture. I have a Spanish friend in Madrid who was one of the classmates at the English language school in Kent, England where I studied for four weeks in 1988. I wish I could trip or stay abroad for 46 days. My husband is not so patient as Bill. This last summer I traveled in England and Scotland for 12 days, but he complained about it at that time. He doesn't want to go with me because he hates the airplane. He retired in May at the age of 60 but still works at a different office. I'm working at the same school as before teaching 5/6th mornings.

My second daughter Mari will marry next April. Emi, first daughter still lives in Nagoya with her husband. My son Koichi has two jobs now, one is dance instructor and the other is to do customer's service belonging to an internet providing company. He is 27 and manages to make his own living. He lives in an apartment in Simokitazawa, Shibuya ward.

I'm concerned about your arthritis in your neck. Have you recovered from it? Take good care and don't work too hard, please I do hope you and Bill and your family are all keeping well. Have a brilliant Chritmas time. Hoping to see you in the near future.

Lots of love, Kikue.

IN CLOSING   FIRST A WEDDING PAGE OR TWO OR?

NANCY AND GORD in Santa Ana, California with SARAH AND DON.

NANCY AND GORD'S RECEPTION IN THUNDER BAY

MIKE AND STACY TOPOROWSKI at the top;
ANNE AND BEN JOHNSON

GREG AND MEG KREWSKI on Galiano Island

I've missed out a lot of important events that happened after I came back from Our Cabana in Mexico. Kori Cuthbert was born in 1989, Kelly Cuthbert was born in 1991. Marcia Dheilly-Sturrock was born in 1997 and Matthew Dheilly-Sturrock in 1999. These are my grandchildren [don't forget Randi Cuthbert born in 1987]. Each of them has a special spot in my heart. I have watched their journeys closely and cheered their many successes. I'm proud of them and the guidance their parents gave them.

THOSE CUTHBERT KIDS.

AND THE DHEILLY-STURROCKS

Bill and I went to Palm Springs for a golfing honeymoon in 1994. It was a break from school routines and a peaceful time together. The following year I went with friends Helen, Marg, and Mary to golf and catch some rays. Bill and I went back to Palm Springs once or twice more in semester breaks.

In the summer we either went to visit Yvette and family in Portage la Prairie, Manitoba or to explore the four corners' [Utah, Arizona, Colorado and Nevada] indigenous sites-some of Lewis and Clark's trails or other historic sites en route to visit Cousin Sarah and Don in Lake Forest, California. We saw most of the South Western States, watched for wildlife; cave or cliff dwellings and huge trees. We camped, cooked some meals on our own, moved along slowly or quickly depending on our moods and the weather. We rarely stayed in hotels.

OUR FAMILIES

We attended friends' and family's weddings, christenings, birthdays and funerals. Whenever Sarah and Don, Yvette or other special guests came we would have an open house so we could invite their relatives and friends. We have always maintained a large social circle.

My sisters, brothers, cousins, Aunts, Uncles, Mom and Dad, all were part of our lives as were their challenges and successes. I value all I have learned from them as well as from my myriad friends and educators. I am a lifelong learner. I have learned a lot from Bill and his family. Sharing with others is so empowering to both sides of the equation.

Yes, I'm a people person busy collecting new friends and taking life's extended course in experiential education. I hope you join me.